SEPTEMBER–DECEMBER 1998

Guidelines

VOLUME 14 / PART 3

Edited by **Grace Emmerson and John Parr**

The Bible Reading Fellowship
OPENING THE BIBLE

Writers in this issue

The Bible and Health **James Woodward** was formerly Chaplain of the Queen Elizabeth Hospital in Birmingham. He is now Priest-in-Charge of Middleton and Wishaw, and the Bishop of Birmingham's Advisor for Health and Social Care.

Nehemiah **Philip Jenson** is a regular contributor to *Guidelines*. He teaches Old Testament at Trinity Theological College, Bristol, having studied in Cambridge, New York and Jerusalem. He is particularly concerned with the rich implications of the Old Testament for the worship and life of the Church, and has published several books on Old Testament subjects.

Lazarus and the Rich Man **Kenneth Bailey** is an ordained minister of the Presbyterian Church (USA). He spent 35 years living and teaching in Egypt, Lebanon, Jerusalem and Cyprus. He specializes in the cultural background and literary forms of the New Testament, and has written and lectured extensively in this field.

Psalms **Harry Mowvley** was formerly Deputy Principal of Bristol Baptist College and Special Lecturer in the University of Bristol. He is the author of several works on the Old Testament.

John 7–12 **John Parr** is priest-in-charge of Harston with Hauxton and Newton, near Cambridge, and Continuing Ministerial Education Officer in the Ely Diocese.

Lamentations **John Goldingay** is Professor of Old Testament Studies at Fuller Theological Seminary in Pasadena, California. Previously he was Principal of St John's College, Nottingham. He has written a number of books on the Old Testament, including some retellings of Old Testament stories called *After Eating the Apricot*. He is married to Ann, who has multiple sclerosis and is disabled, and they have two sons and dughters-in-law.

The Letters of John **John Proctor** is a Minister of the United Reformed Church. After parish work in Glasgow, he now teaches New Testament studies in the Cambridge Theological Federation. He is married to Elaine, with two teenage children.

Christmas Readings **Christopher Rowland** is Dean Ireland's Professor of the Exegesis of Holy Scripture in the University of Oxford. He was formerly joint editor of Guidelines and is the author of many books, including a new commentary on the book of Revelation, and takes a keen interest in issues of justice in Britain and the Third World.

THE BRF Magazine

The BRF Prayer

O God our Father,
in the holy scriptures
you have given us your word
to be our teacher and guide:
help us and all the members of our Fellowship
to seek in our reading
the guidance of the Holy Spirit
that we may learn more of you
and of your will for us,
and so grow in likeness to your Son,
Jesus Christ our Lord.
Amen.

Editors' Letter

This issue of *Guidelines* contains the usual rich mixture of biblical material. The Old Testament readings encompass story and poetry, action and meditation, triumph and disaster. First we have Nehemiah defiantly rebuilding the ruined walls of Jerusalem and confronting the scorn and treachery of enemies posing as would-be friends. Later we meditate on the psalms, our emotions engaged and our commitment challenged by those ancient poets. Finally we share in the anguished outpourings of grief found in the book of Lamentations and marvel at the courage which, in the face of immense suffering, can still cling to the faith that 'the steadfast love of the Lord never ceases'. These ancient texts find many an echo in today's world, as individuals and nations struggle to rebuild their ruined lives, and out of their anguish create a future.

As a counterpoint to Lamentations' theme of suffering, we begin this issue with two weeks of readings on 'The Bible and Health'. Here you will find biblical perspectives on an issue that is of great importance to all human beings. Those of you who prefer shorter daily readings will be glad of a whole fortnight devoted to one of the best-known parables in the gospels, Jesus' story of the Rich Man and Lazarus in Luke 16. The parable is read alongside several other biblical passages, mostly from the New Testament. The second instalment of readings from John's Gospel covers chapters 7–12. As the conflict between Jesus and the Jewish leaders intensifies, Jesus emerges as the one who retains control over his destiny. We continue with the Johannine writings during the first part of Advent, as we read the Letters of John. Their incarnational theology is very appropriate as we prepare to celebrate Christmas. This year's Christmas readings cover familiar ground, without allowing the seasonal message of reassurance and hope to crowd out some of the disturbing features of the Christmas story.

We continue to be very encouraged by the letters we receive from readers. A consistent theme is the importance of Guidelines in the pilgrimage of faith. For us, and all the staff at BRF, it is gratifying, if also humbling, to realize that our work can be used to nourish faith in this way. Do please keep writing, and thank you for your continued support and interest.

With best wishes.

Grace Emmerson, John Parr
Guidelines Editors

Richard Fisher writes...

It's always difficult to know exactly how to approach this column in *The BRF Magazine*. You will read these words seven or eight months after they were written, and so what appears topical now may seem far less so then.

Looking back

We have just come to the end of 1997 and our 75th anniversary year. And what a year it turned out to be. Little did anyone imagine as we sat in Westminster Abbey for our Service of Thanksgiving in January that the world's attention would be focused here one Saturday morning eight months later for the funeral of Diana, Princess of Wales.

And little did anyone at the BRF service listening to Shelagh Brown read from 2 Timothy think that we would lose her six months later as the result of a fall at home.

So 1997 was a year of great sadness, but also of great joy. It was a pleasure to meet so many of our readers and supporters at the various 75th anniversary events and celebrations that took place throughout the year. Two of the many highlights were the retreats led by Gerard W. Hughes and John Went, Bishop of Tewkesbury. We now plan to have an ongoing programme of retreats, beginning this autumn. If you would like to receive details of these please send an A5 s.a.e. marked 'Retreats' in the top left corner.

We are living in an age that is more spiritually aware than ever before

Looking forward

The millennium is fast approaching. Plans are afoot for all kinds of lavish celebrations and events. But do these have any meaning? Ask most people exactly what it is we're going to celebrate and they haven't the first idea. At the same time there is recognition that we are living in an age that is more spiritually aware than ever before. This is such an opportunity for the

Church—we can give *meaning* to the millennium event. Here is a chance to proclaim the gospel and to share with others the life, ministry and teaching of Jesus, as we move into the third millennium after his birth. As Bishop James Jones stated in his sermon at the BRF 75th anniversary service in January 1997: 'To celebrate Jesus' life without reference to the scriptures would be like commemorating Shakespeare without staging his plays. The millennium has no substance without scripture.' With our range of Bible reading notes (and our other resources), we can help people to read and understand the Bible. And as they come to the written word, so we pray they will encounter the living word, Jesus Christ himself. As we draw closer to the millennium, will you help us to introduce others to the Bible? Will you help us to make them aware of the ways BRF can help them to read it regularly?

The millennium has no substance without scripture

New Publications

We have published a new volume in the *Day by Day* series as a tribute to Shelagh Brown. *Day by Day with Shelagh Brown* includes some of the best of her readings from *New Daylight*, arranged in themes. A donation from the sale of every copy will go to support the work of TEARFUND. The new Advent book for 1998 is *On the way to Bethlehem* by Hilary McDowell and an extract from this can be found on page 15. And on page 20 you can read about *Cracking the church cocoon*, an imaginative new resource for evangelism and outreach in the local church.

BRF publishes up to 35 new books each year. If you would like to receive our catalogue and information about BRF resources on a regular basis, please write and let us know.

And finally

Thank you for your many positive and encouraging letters about *The BRF Magazine*.

We hope you will find the combination of articles, features and book extracts in this issue both interesting and informative. And of course we hope and pray that you will continue to enjoy your daily Bible reading notes.

P.S. We shall be at the Christian Resources Exhibition at the NEC in Birmingham (11 — 14 November). If you are able to visit the exhibition, do come and see us on stand number 128/229.

An Emmaus Walk

Brother Ramon SSF

The Emmaus Walk is an exercise in which prayer and scripture run together in a walking meditation. The specific goal of this exercise is for two believers to walk together in fellowship and in silence, allowing the risen Christ to minister within and between them. It begins in a group meeting, providing the context of silence, scripture and prayer, then breaks up into couples for the actual Emmaus Walk, and returns about an hour later to share the experiences of the walk, and to offer it to God in gratitude and praise.

I introduced this exercise for our Franciscan friars and sisters some years ago, and it has spread to churches, schools, prayer groups and retreatants with enthusiasm. It is simple, biblical, and has the virtue of providing both input and feedback.

Simple, biblical, providing both input and feedback

On one memorable occasion I shared it with a young people's group at Tymawr convent. We put our names into a hat and I was paired with Luke, who was then eighteen years of age. On the silent return walk it became quite clear to me that the Lord had a specific word for him, and it unfolded itself as we walked quietly together. We had five minutes in hand, and sat on a wall, conscious of the Lord's presence and blessing.

I did not communicate the 'word' to Luke during the later shared session, but wrote it out for him so that he could refer to it, and then we talked it through. It was a significant 'word for the future' which has since stood him in good stead in times of difficulty and conflict. He is now into the fifth year of ordination training, and he keeps in touch. We both remember our Emmaus Walk with great joy.

I shall now describe the exercise simply, and then include the original pattern, which has been used for the basis of the Emmaus Walk. One and a half or two hours are needed for the walk, including the time spent together before and after the exercise. The group meets together for the first section, breaking into pairs for the walk (pairing is best decided by names in a hat to enable a good mix), and all return to the central place at an agreed time to share experiences and conclude the session in prayer.

You can introduce your own variations—for instance, it may be thought best to begin together, do the walk, but then to arrange a separate evening to meet for the pooling of experiences, for there may be an enthusiastic outpouring! I shall outline it as for our own community, and then variations may be made according to the needs of a particular group.

Introduction

'Were not our hearts burning within us while he was talking to us on the road, while he was opening the scriptures to us?' (Luke 24:32)

The group meets in a church or quiet place, and all the participants' names are put into a bowl. The leader selects and reads them out in pairs for the walk. After five minutes of settling into a relaxed silence, there is a prayer and reading as follows:

INVOCATION (THE FOLLOWING, OR AN EXTEMPORE PRAYER):

Lord Jesus Christ: Grant us now a sense of your loving presence, and by the light of your Holy Spirit open our minds to your love. As the hearts of the Emmaus walkers burned within them so long ago, so may your loving presence be the source of warmth and light to us as we walk with you and reflect on your word. And to you be thanks and praise, in the glory of the Father and the unity of the Holy Spirit. Amen.

SCRIPTURE (EXAMPLES AS FOLLOWS):

Luke 24:13–35	Emmaus walk
Matthew 4:1–11	Temptation
Matthew 4:18–25	Call and healing
Matthew 5:1–14	Jesus' teaching
Matthew 5:38–48	The way of love

Appropriate to Lent/Passiontide:

Matthew 26:31–35, 69–75	Peter's denial
John 21:15–19	Peter's restoration
Matthew 26:36–56	Gethsemane/arrest
Matthew 27:11–31	Trial and mocking
Matthew 27:32–56	Crucifixion

Some modern translations supply a table of parables and miracles of Jesus. Almost any such passage is suitable for meditative reading at this point.

COMMENTARY ON THE READING, POETRY, ETC.

FIVE MINUTES OF SHARED SILENCE

The Walk

The outward walk should take half an hour, and the aim should be a prayerful sharing on the basis of the scripture/commentary read, with freedom to move into any other areas of common concern.

When the outward point has

been reached, the pair should pause, turn, and retrace their steps together, but now in silence (steady pace!) There should be an open awareness of one another and of the risen Christ's promised presence.

Conclusion

Return to the quiet place.

If desired, re-read the scripture or the second part of an agreed passage, (e.g. if Peter's denial has been read, then Peter's restoration can now be read).

There may be an open sharing of any experiences that any of the participants may have felt during the walk.Spend at least a further five minutes in silence, perhaps followed by a hymn or music.

> *Only in a relationship of loving trust can Christ manifest himself*

The Emmaus Walk exercise is meant to provide a simple way of sharing with another, something of the experience that occurred on the road to Emmaus in Luke 24:13–35. In order to be silent with another, there needs to be a great measure of trust and openness. Only in a relationship of such loving trust can Christ manifest himself. When this happens, there is immense joy—and sometimes profound wonder.

But a warning note needs to be sounded. This walk must not be undertaken lightly without due preparation and prayer. Silence in solitude or shared with another can expose a person to the light and scrutiny of God, and the result could be either a sense of fear at being so exposed, or an experience of embarrassment and the inability to share or cope.

If prayerful preparation has been undertaken, and the first experience doesn't altogether succeed, don't let that worry you. There is a novelty factor that has to be worked through, and temperamental differences to be allowed for. Persistence, and allowing for one another, are part of this exercise. One grows into shared silence, and what began as a novelty, or as an embarrassing non-verbal walk, can turn out to be a fruitful sharing of a love that transcends human friendship and participates in the divine Love.

Collect and Grace

Lord Jesus Christ: We thank you for your presence with us on our pilgrimage, for our time together and for all we have received from your hand. Enable us to carry your healing presence to our brothers and sisters, and ever to walk with you, until the day of your appearing, in the glory of the Father, and the unity of the Holy Spirit. Amen.

(Together) The grace of our Lord Jesus Christ, and the love of God, and the fellowship of the Holy Spirit be with us evermore. Amen.

An Interview with Graham Usher

It was a chance encounter in Israel with the late Shelagh Brown that first sparked Graham Usher's interest in the Bible Reading Fellowship. He had been working in the area of Jewish–Christian relations when he happened to meet her—and although the meeting was brief, the impression she left was lasting.

'Meeting her had a very strong impact on my life,' he recalls. 'It was her outrageous sense of fun combined with a very deep holiness, an exceptional combination of qualities in one person. She also had an acute sense of what was happening in the world.'

On Shelagh's recommendation, Graham was appointed as a BRF Trustee. Sadly, he did not take his place on the Council until the summer following her death. Nevertheless, he remains much enthused for the role of BRF in Christian life today:

'BRF offers a challenge for people to turn the pages of scripture and really explore what is there. It allows them the chance to marinade, if you like, in the Bible. And this is something which is being lost from society, especially among the younger generation.'

Graham, 28, brings to the role of Trustee a special concern for people in their 20s and 30s, and is also a national trustee of the Scout Association and is involved with the Duke of Edinburgh Award Scheme in the North East.

Since June 1996, he has been a curate at the church of St Mary the Virgin, Nunthorpe, in York diocese, living there with his wife Rachel who is a GP. He describes himself as 'half Scottish, half Welsh and all Yorkshire'!

Before his three years of ministerial training in Cambridge, where he gained a theology degree, he studied Ecological Science at Edinburgh University. He still teaches at an Edinburgh summer school on nature conservation in Scotland, and the link between theology and conservation of the natural world is one that interests him greatly.

Give us today our daily bread

John Fenton

The Lord's Prayer, in Matthew's version (6:9–13), begins with three petitions: that God will act to hallow his name; that he will begin to rule; and that his will will be done—throughout the whole of his creation. To say this part of the prayer is to fulfil what is commanded later in the Sermon on the Mount: 'Strive first for the kingdom of God and his righteousness, and all these things [food, drink and clothing] will be given to you as well' (6:33).

The prayer asks that God will act quickly

The second part of the prayer consists of petitions that relate to the first part and follow on from what was said there; because when God rules over the world, we want to be included in the kingdom. Moreover, it is of course taken for granted by those who say the prayer that life will then be far better than it is now; so the prayer asks that God will act quickly, and make the change-over from this age to the age to come, immediately. This is similar to the ending of Revelation: 'The one who testifies to these things [i.e. Jesus; see Revelation 1:1] says, "Surely I am coming soon." Amen. Come, Lord Jesus!' (22:20).

When the books of the New Testament were being written, most of those who wrote them, and most of those for whom they were written, must have been living in discomfort and insecurity; hatred and persecution were never far away. So those who said the Lord's Prayer would have been longing for the coming of the new age, the time when there would be no more evil and suffering.

If we remember this, it may help us to understand the original meaning of the first petition in the second part of the prayer. We ask God to give us bread, and that we may have it today. The word 'today' is the last word in the petition; and, in Greek, the last word in a sentence is often where the emphasis lies. We could translate the Greek, using the same order of words, to make the same point: our ???? bread—give it to us, today.

It means, Do not let things go on as they have done in the past; change everything, by giving us our bread. And do this, today, immediately.

But we have missed out two words, where the ???? comes. The prayer does not only say 'our bread'; it describes it, using a Greek word; and no one knows for certain what this Greek word means. It was, apparently, a rare word at the time when Matthew was writing his gospel; in the New Testament it comes only twice, here and in Luke 11:3, which is the Lucan version of the Lord's Prayer. A century later, the word had dropped out of use altogether, apart from its presence in this prayer, and in discussions about the meaning of the prayer. Most people in the past have taken it to mean 'daily', but more recent studies of the prayer favour the idea that it means something more like 'the future', 'tomorrow'. So the New Revised Standard Version (NRSV) has 'our daily bread' in the text, but 'our bread for tomorrow' in the margin; similarly, the Revised English Bible (REB) also has 'our daily bread' in the text, but 'our bread for the morrow' as the alternative. (There is an excellent discussion of this, and of the Lord's Prayer as a whole, in the recently republished book *The Lord's Prayer* by C.F. Evans, SCM Press 1997).

The age to come was sometimes described as a feast

The age to come was sometimes described as a feast (e.g. Matthew 8:11), or a wedding banquet (Revelation 19:9), an occasion for eating and drinking ('Happy are those who will sit at the feast in the kingdom of God', Luke 14:15, REB). This was why the meals of Jesus, described in the gospels, and the feeding-miracles, were so important for the first readers of these books; they were anticipations of the future.

There is another passage in the Old Testament that may also be part of the background of this part of the Lord's Prayer. The idea of asking today for the bread for tomorrow, may recall the account of the manna in Exodus 16, and in particular the supply of the bread for the Sabbath on the day before the Sabbath (16:22–26). Once again, the meaning would be: Make today the sixth day, and make tomorrow the final sabbath, the time of everlasting life.

With all of this in mind, what might we think, as we say this

...continued on page 19

On the Way to Bethlehem

Hilary McDowell

The latest book from popular *New Daylight* and *Day by Day with God* contributor Hilary McDowell is BRF's Advent book for 1998: *On the Way to Bethlehem*. It aims to take the reader on a spiritual journey of discovery, putting the wonder back into a season so often burdened by pressures of work, money, gift-buying, or family relationships.

Hilary uses the well-loved BRF pattern of daily Bible readings, together with a passage of comment and a point for reflection or a prayer. But by combining well-known Advent scriptures with Bible passages less commonly associated with this time of year, she has written a particularly fresh and imaginative series of readings in her own unique style.

In search of the Christ child we travel expectantly

As she herself puts it: 'In search of the Christ child we leave the familiar and travel expectantly, open to the possibility of God surprising us along the way. The destination is God's choosing, the itinerary etched by the Bible, the search is for Jesus.'

Hilary is a well-known author and all-round communicator, as well as a Presbyterian deaconess, despite coping with numerous disabilities since birth. She has also written *Some Day I'm Going to Fly* (Triangle 1995) and *Around the World on Eighty Prayers* (Triangle 1997).

The following extract presents a day's reading from the first section of *On the Way to Bethlehem*, entitled 'Packing the Case'.

Section 1: Packing the case

THE DECISION TO JOURNEY

Read Genesis 1:1–3. 'Let there be light.'

A choice lay ahead. The traveller could allow herself to be dragged towards Bethlehem, this year, kicking and screaming through the tinsel-laden pressures of the expected route to Christmas. Already her local radio station had been announcing the countdown of the days even before the leaves had started to fall. Was the world getting crazier, or was it just her?

Would she journey or not? All around her, folk were expressing the desire to stay at home, lock all doors, put the phone off the hook and 'opt out' of the pandemonium. After all, hadn't she 'been there, bought the T-shirt', year after year?

On the other hand, suppose she hadn't seen it all? Supposing God could surprise her? What if there was something at the destination more than shopping aisles and carols and mince-pies?

She was already fed up with the shortening, dark, old days before Christmas, with their impending sanity-free workload of preparation, the anticipation of reaching the new year with a deep desire to lie in a darkened room until spring. There was altogether too much darkness, in more ways than one.

Yes, she would go. Right from Genesis he had promised light, and she owed it to herself to make the journey. What she dreaded was packing the case.

Drag the luggage from below the bed and set it out for a good airing—slightly musty from months of disuse. Will it be big enough to hold all the necessaries? Let's see—she selected the most favourite clothes, the ones that made her feel and look the best. Then in went the protection from the sun, protection from cold, and lots of underwear.

Better not be caught out financially, she thought. Cheque book, cash, identification for border crossings, and passport. Extra insurance for loss of luggage, time, personal injury, just in case. Followed by maps, instructions, repair kit, first-aid box. An expanding bag or two would not go amiss, and the hold-all and shopping bag and…

What a weight to carry, she thought, but kept stacking. She packed for the weather she expected, the enjoyment she craved, the 'image' to be created. Of course the emotional and psychological baggage packed itself automatically. It was all in there, past experiences and learned strategies. Fears from yesterday's wounds and failures, bad memories and good ones.

GENESIS 37:1–4

Jacob dwelt in the land of his father's sojournings, in the land of Canaan. This is the history of the family of Jacob.

Joseph, being seventeen years old, was shepherding the flock with his brothers; he was a lad with the sons of Bihah and Zilpah, his father's wives; and Joseph brought an ill report of them to their father. Now Israel loved Joseph more than any other of his children, because he was the son of his old age; and he made him a long robe with sleeves. But when his brothers saw that their father loved him more than all his brothers, they hated him, and could not speak peaceably to him.

Joseph gathered a heavy burden of luggage early in life. A favourite child with the privileges and the jealousies that come with such a position. A spoilt child with a great deal more than a many-coloured coat, but the coat didn't help the situation as such a garment, in the culture of the day, denoted a favour which was normally the right of the eldest son. Then, to add insult to injury, the favouritism nurtured in him arrogance, detestable to his brothers. At seventeen, he was 'sneaking' to his father about their behaviour. His journey of life burdened him early with some very heavy luggage indeed.

Traveller, as we step out towards Bethlehem this year, it's good to take time to examine what is packed in the old suitcase. Items hidden there from years of hurts and wounds and jealousies and anger and unforgiveness. We need to cleanse our expectations of the journey, open ourselves to God's itinerary, relinquish our 'image' of ourselves, whether that be good or bad. Joseph wasn't planning to go anywhere; as far as he was concerned, he'd arrived! Will our traveller begin her Advent journey making the same mistake?

Dear God,

It's hard to prepare for the journey with a fresh spirit. Been here before, we think.

Father, ruffle my packing enough to help me see the vision you have for me along the way.

Please gift me with the right amount of wonder for anticipation, a healthy degree of trepidation to know I travel in the hands of a living God who can touch my yesterdays as much as my tomorrows. Lord, make me expectant, make me new. Amen

The New Lectionary

Trevor Lloyd and Rachel Boulding

By the time we reach the millennium, many of the main churches in Britain—and throughout the English-speaking world—will be reading the same Bible passages every Sunday. Churches are switching to a three-year cycle, the Revised Common Lectionary, which is an ecumenical revision of the Roman Catholic Common Lectionary, adapted for use in a wide range of churches. In the Church of England, it is becoming known as the Common Worship Lectionary, after the overall title for the new services which are appearing over the next few years.

It covers Sundays and festivals only—not ordinary weekdays—offering Old Testament, New Testament, Psalm and Gospel readings for each chosen day, and has several advantages over previous schemes. It offers more scope by covering more of the Bible, giving the chance to read books of the Old and New Testaments continuously, over a period of time, in order to get a sense of each book's integrity.

It offers the chance to read books of the Old and New Testaments continuously

For the Church of England, for example, the new approach involves a change from the earlier way of reading scripture in the *Alternative Service Book 1980*. This was guided by the choice of a special theme for each Sunday. When the *Alternative Service Book* first appeared, many people welcomed the themes' freshness, but over the years two problems emerged. The subjects were very varied ('The Proof of Faith', 'The Ascension of Christ', 'The Serving Community', and so on), but some of them could seem narrow after being used a few times; they wore thin. The other, more serious, difficulty was that there was a danger of scripture coming to be read through predetermined themes, rather than with the openness and expectation that looks to see what it is saying to the people.

These difficulties reflect the differences between the two main ways that most lectionaries have been put together over the centuries. The thematic approach, if linked with different seasons of the year, could at least have the benefit of focusing on the main festivals of the Church, such as Christmas and Easter, with readings reflecting first Christ's birth and then his death and resurrection. But this could be taken too far and the themes could become a straitjacket for congregations and preachers.

The new lectionary offers a rich and varied diet

In contrast to this, there is a semi-continuous approach (*lectio continua* if you want to be academic). This involves reading right through whole books of the Bible with as few interruptions as possible for seasons and festivals. This is the approach taken by Thomas Cranmer, architect of the *Book of Common Prayer*, at the Reformation, and also by the *Revised Common Lectionary*. The three years of the cycle are referred to as A, B and C. Each one focuses on a different synoptic gospel, with the Gospel of John spread over all the years. It is worth looking more closely at how this works in practice.

Year A starts in Advent (December) 1998 and runs to the end of November 1999. This focuses on the Gospel of Matthew. During Advent, the Old Testament reading is from Isaiah, illuminating the gospel readings about the coming of Christ, and the second readings come from Romans and 1 Corinthians. From Ash Wednesday to Pentecost, while Matthew remains the focus, there are some of the traditional readings from John's Gospel during the last three Sundays of Lent and the Easter season.

Year B runs from Advent 1999 to the end of November 2000. This focuses on the Gospel of Mark. During Advent, the New Testament readings come mainly from the two letters to the Corinthians, while from Ash Wednesday to Pentecost the New Testament readings are a semi-continuous reading from 1 John. The first readings come from Acts during the Easter season in Year B, instead of from the Old Testament.

Year C runs from Advent 2000 to the end of November 2001. This focuses on the Gospel of Luke, again with readings from John coming in during the Ash Wednesday to Pentecost season. After Easter, there are semi-continuous readings from Revelation. After Pentecost, Jeremiah figures largely in the Old

Testament reading with semi-continuous selections from Galatians, Colossians, 1 and 2 Timothy, and 2 Thessalonians. As in other years, the final Sundays after Pentecost focus on the second coming and the reign of Christ.

The new lectionary offers a rich and varied diet, covering more of the whole Bible than other schemes in a systematic way. As a way of encountering God Sunday by Sunday, it should stimulate growth in our churches—and in our lives.

Trevor Lloyd *is the Archdeacon of Barnstaple and a member of the Church of England's Liturgical Commission.* **Rachel Boulding** *is Liturgy Editor at Church House Publishing.*

The Bible passages for the Sunday readings in New Daylight *are all taken from the Revised Common Lectionary.*

Give us today our daily bread

Continued from page 13

petition, 'Give us today our bread for the morrow'? Perhaps something like this: when God finally brings us to himself, we shall see in complete clarity that we are and always have been totally dependent upon him. 'You created all things; by your will they were created and have their being!' (Revelation 4:11) We want to see this now, and to live in the light of this understanding, already, today. We want the reality of God to break through the darkness of our minds. We keep forgetting the truth, and imagining that the world has no God, but runs itself. Make us see our dependence on you; the bread by which we exist is your will and purpose. Help us to believe in you.

A contemporary writer, Morar Lucas, has put this in a short poem:

'Give us this day our daily bread'
consider what this means:
first, wholemeal, sliced and granary,
hot rolls and buns and beans.

And more—we ask the world to come
to illuminate today:
not less than the Eternal Word—
for this we dare to pray.

As members of the Wedding Feast,
rejoicing and forgiven,
accept in awestruck confidence
God's gift, the Bread of Heaven.

Chrysalis: cracking the church cocoon

Creative evangelism through the performing arts

Calling all Christians who would like to provide a bridge for those unfamiliar with the church environment but don't know where to start!

Cracking the church cocoon is BRF's exciting new handbook designed to help your church put on a non-threatening, entertaining yet informative evangelistic event.

This 160-page A4 book is packed with all the background information you need to stage an outreach event; from grounding the vision in prayer and study, to choosing the venue, speakers and programme, and organizing the technical back-up.

Cracking the church cocoon grew from the vision of two professional singers who wanted to offer an innovative and powerful cabaret-style first step introduction to the gospel. Together they built an outreach programme of events, called *Chrysalis*.

This is followed by nine complete thematic programmes, all of which have been performed by the *Chrysalis* team:

The Truth about Love
The Truth about Power
The Truth about Suffering
The Truth about Money
The Truth about Christianity
The Truth about Sex
The Truth about the Bible
The Truth about Freedom
The Truth about Christmas

Their learnt experience forms the basis for the first section of this book, including:

1. *In the beginning...*
2. *Grounding the vision and gathering the troops*
3. *Teams, themes and theology*
4. *Programming—format, timing, elements*
5. *The power of music*
6. *Drama*
7. *Arabesques, doggerels and other assorted art forms*
8. *Personal testimonies*
9. *The talk—speaking to seekers*
10. *Technical considerations*
11. *Presentation*
12. *Publicity*

Each thematic programme includes:

Bible passages and study guides which ground the theme

Designed to help your church to get to grips with the teaching that undergirds the theme, and to learn together as you prepare the programme.

Programme outline

A clear and useful breakdown of a typical programme based on the theme, to help you build your programme.

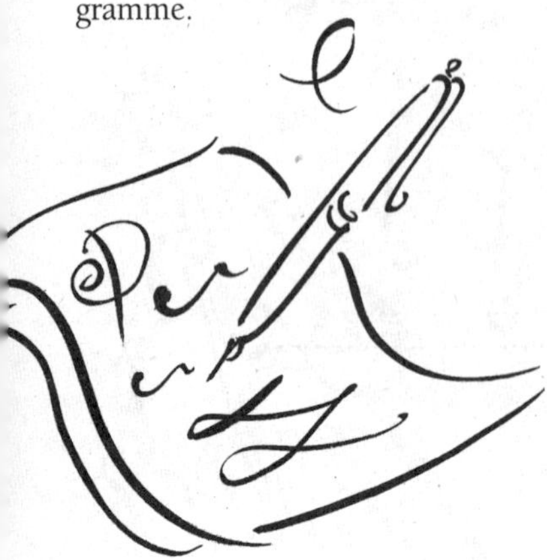

Drama sketches

Nine original sketches, expertly written and easy to perform.

Music lyrics and scores

Nine original songs, complete with full lyrics, simple notation and guitar chords. Full scores and CD available from *Chrysalis Arts Trust*.

Poetry

Thematic verse to fit into your programme.

Outline of the talk including Bible passages, bulleted summary, quotable quotes and timeless illustrations

A comprehensive framework, based on carefully researched and field-tested material, to help you build an evangelistic talk.

Section on resources specific to the theme

A useful selection of organizations supplying everything from technical equipment to CDs and cassettes.

Both authors are founder members of *Chrysalis* and the *Chrysalis Arts Trust*.

Mandy Watsham is a full-time musician working primarily in Christian music ministry. She has toured with the internationally renowned Continental Singers and is the vocal coach for British Youth for Christ. She has won many awards for her singing, including double honours for her portrayal of the Queen of the Night from Mozart's *Magic Flute*.

Nicki Matthews is director of programming for *Chrysalis*. She has professionally directed and choreographed for many different companies and often performs in concerts and musical shows, encompassing a variety of musical styles.

Illustrations are by Ian Mitchell.

The authors write:

The universal language of the performing arts—music, drama and the spoken word—is an effective formula for presenting the gospel to those beyond the fringe of the church. Many churches recognize this fact and the need to meet people on their own ground, yet feel overwhelmed by the enormity of the task.

Chrysalis was formed in 1992 with the sole purpose of using the performing arts to take the message of the Christian gospel out of the church and into the familiar, relaxed surroundings of the local football club or pub. Five years on, the Chrysalis concept has moved from strength to strength, taking its programme of non-threatening, biblically-based events to churches seeking to minister to those outside their normal congregation. It is an excellent springboard into Alpha and similar programmes.

Fiona Castle writes:

'I am excited to see talented Christian performers using their gifts to spread the message of the gospel. Their professionalism… should ensure that this type of creative outreach makes a tremendous impact on today's society.'

Lee Strobel, author, speaker and teaching pastor at Willow Creek Community Church, writes:

'I am praying that God will bless the efforts of musicians, actors, and other artists as they creatively bring Christ's message of hope to people who desperately need it.'

***Cracking the church cocoon* is designed to enable you to use the Chrysalis concept as a whole, or simply to select the material which best suits your situation and tailor it to your need.**

The Bible and Health

Over the next fortnight we shall be looking at some biblical passages which deal with the issues surrounding health and wholeness. The first week's readings offer some biblical perspectives on health, and in the second week we shall be asking who takes responsibility for our health.

The notes can be used with any translation of the Bible.

31 AUGUST–6 SEPTEMBER PERSPECTIVES

1 Our healing ministry *Read James 5:13–18*

This is the only detailed reference to such practice for healing within a liturgical framework. With a sense of confidence and energy it offers us a pattern to explore and implement. Within this framework, healing can include the deliverance from physical disease and the restoration of strength (v. 15). This healing is linked to the forgiveness of sin and a deep concern for people's state of mind (vv. 13 and 15).

There are three elements within the framework. The first is that this ministry involves everyone. On occasions it includes the elders or leaders of the congregation (v. 16). But equally, the ordinary members of the congregation supporting and caring for one another exercise this ministry (v. 14). The second element is prayer. Undergirding this is a belief that prayer works (v. 16) when it is earnest and believing (v. 15), and when it is specifically for the need in hand (v. 16), meaning a specific request or petition. This request carries no faith requirement and does not guarantee cure (v. 16). It includes confession and forgiveness, which both have a potential role in healing and involves remembering to thank God (v. 13). The third element is anointing with oil (v. 14), which was commonly used in Jesus' day. This may have a dual purpose. It could imply a specific religious act, and may also recognize the common practice of using oil in contemporary medical practice. So verse 14 could be translated as 'let them pray over him, giving him his medical treatment in the name of the Lord.'

This framework will provide the basis for our reflections on the Bible and health. It encourages us to have a concern for the sick and to regard healing as part of the ministry of the Church. Within this ministry prayer plays a significant role, and healing ministry includes a variety of activities: physical, spiritual, medical and corporate. There is a role both for spontaneity and organization. And sickness has mental, social and spiritual aspects—the whole person is involved. Cure is not something guaranteed, but there is an expectation that something positive will happen. Finally there is a community dimension to healing—the provision of a loving, caring and healing environment.

2 The role of intercessory prayer *Read Luke 11:1–13*

The request 'Lord, teach us to pray' has been made many times since the occasion it was asked of Jesus and his disciples. Part of our witness is to heed what the Bible can give us to enrich our lives about the place of prayer.

Intercessory prayer is often seen as a kind of pleading with God or as our telling God all that we would wish him to do. Sometimes the Intercessions in church can sound like our shopping list, or a summary of the local and national news bulletin. Perhaps our Intercessions should be more as Jesus directed.

In the privacy and silence of our own hearts and lives we are asked to wait on the God who knows us and cherishes us. Our peace and health are at least in part connected with the recognition that we have a Father who is always more ready to give than we are to receive. Intercession, then, becomes a placing of ourselves and others within the love of God. In praise and gratitude we affirm the power of God's healing. In stillness and humility we bring to God places and people in need of healing and peace.

3 The struggle against evil in the pursuit of health *Read Luke 11:14–26*

There are several misunderstandings about demons and demon possession. Some Christians are tempted to see demons everywhere, and others to dismiss Satan as a construct of a former and less enlightened age. Our attitudes to demons can sometimes take the edge off the critical nature of our daily encounter with evil in both its individual and more corporate forms. In all our lives there are times when we are confronted by a sudden upsurge of evil. When we are unprepared we can be left battered, bruised and shaken.

When it was suggested to Jesus that he drove out demons by the power of Beelzebul, the prince of demons, he countered by saying that this would mean something inconceivable, namely that Satan was divided against himself. A kingdom divided against itself is laid waste and a divided household cannot stand. His works of healing were the result of intervention by a higher power, the finger of God.

This image of the divided household suggests the need for integration: wholeness of body, mind and spirit. It also challenges us towards a renewal in relationships, with God, our neighbour and our whole environment. On Calvary, evil was defeated by this sacrifice of love. However, that does not relieve us of responsibility for the reality of evil both in and around us. True healing, and the healing of the world, may then depend upon how far we can become so identified with Christ. In this identification we can be empowered to withstand and engage with the continuing pressures of evil and ensure that love always has the final word.

4 God's presence as a key to healthy living

Read Luke 11:27–28

There is an important prelude to this brief encounter. Jesus had been teaching and healing and, as usual, produced a mixed reaction. Some people were astonished, others demanded an authenticating sign; and some accused him of being demonic. Why is it that so many have failed, and still fail, to acknowledge his healing power? This unnamed woman in the crowd recognized the divine in him, and shouted out a blessing on the mother who bore and bred him. Many commentators have dismissed her outburst. Some even suggest that Jesus repudiated it as extravagant emotionalism and empty piety.

Isn't that rather harsh? Did she not sense the unique gift of God in the words and works of Jesus? Was this not her way of giving praise for all that Jesus was doing and saying?

Jesus wanted her (and us) to go further. He pronounced a blessing on those who hear God's word and keep, or do, it. When Jesus is present and received, God's word is heard, and faith may lead to action. In our understanding of health the divine presence becomes a key to healthy living.

5 Miracles are not the be-all and end-all *Read Luke 11:29–32*

Jonah had been the subject of a miraculous deliverance from death by God and that was why the people of Nineveh listened to him and repented. Jesus himself performed miracles and therefore was greater than Jonah.

The healing miracles of Jesus had a threefold significance which is indicated by three different words. First, they were *works* done on and for sick people. They solved the immediate problems of their sickness and restored them to a greater measure of health than they knew before. Secondly, they were *wonders*, and made people think, for they had never seen anything like them. Thirdly, they were *signs* which pointed beyond themselves and showed the one who performed them to be more than just a preacher. Jesus was a healer whose healing power came from God and reflected the nature of God. His healing was the practical illustration of the purpose of his preaching.

It was the failure of people to recognize the healing miracles of Jesus as signs that gave him concern. No other sign would be given them until his resurrection from the dead after three days. This is the great healing miracle which is 'our sign of Jonah', by which we know that he is indeed God, who is our saviour and healer.

6 The importance of inner healing *Read Luke 11:37–41*

During a discussion with young children about the eucharist, an eight-year-old came up with an intriguing definition of forgiveness. After appreciating how important it was to prepare for important events, this smart child talked about making sure one's hands and face were clean. 'This forgiveness stuff,' she said, 'must be about getting clean on the inside.'

Being aware of our own needs and encountering the living God who gives us fullness means that we need to attend to and prepare for this mystery.

Jesus reminds us that it is from within that our attitudes come. These attitudes will shape our living and our loving, or our lack of it. It is from within that comes the spark for all our relationships, for good or ill. We pray for healing, wholeness, *shalom*, peace. But peace begins here inside each one of us; with the way we live our lives and pursue our relationships.

We are complex human beings. There is so much within us that needs healing, before we can even begin to look outside. If the dark inside can be brought to the light of God's healing, then his forgiveness and peace can spill over from us to others. Inner healing and our own world of meaning and attitude are a key arena for a wholeness and peace.

GUIDELINES

This week's first reading showed the importance of forgiveness in healing. The parable of the prodigal son in Luke 15:11–32 invites us to consider this further. How would you have reacted if your son had taken all of the money you had provided for him for his future and wasted it? It is easy to overlook the power of the father's response. When he saw his son, he ran out to meet him, embraced him and forgave him everything, and laid on a feast of welcome for him.

The burden of guilt can weigh down on the soul and affect the body. It is always there in depression. Blaming oneself can lead to the contempt of self, self-neglect, self-hate. So receiving and accepting God's forgiveness are essential to good health. Being forgiven by God is accompanied by forgiving others. The unforgiving mind can become the resentful mind, the embittered mind. This too can cause ill health of mind and body. Forgiveness is not easy. Forgiving is an act of the will. Refusing to be avenged, willing others' good and trying to understand them are a profound part of our own and others' health.

1 Jesus asks a question *Read Mark 10:46–52*

Reflect for a moment on the question Jesus asks this man: 'What do you want me to do for you?' From one perspective this is a stupid question to ask a blind man who has called for help. Wouldn't we all know the answer already? Why bother with such a question?

Jesus asks this question for a number of reasons. This man is an outcast of society. Furthermore, we know from the Gospels that many afflictions were regarded by the society of the day as a punishment of the person's, or his/her parents', sin. The prelude to the healing of the man born blind in John's Gospel illustrates this clearly, as Jesus' disciples ask, 'Which man sinned, this man or his parents, that he was born blind?' (John 9:2) If Jesus heals Bartimaeus, his life will be transformed. His place in society will change. It will be costly to him. Jesus wants him to be fully aware of this.

'What do you want me to do for you?' In exploring our own responsibility in the process of health and healing it is important to be aware from the outset that Jesus does not impose himself or his power on people, but always invites them to participate in their own healing.

2 Where true power lies *Read 2 Corinthians 12:7–10*

The Corinthian church was a powerful one with many signs and wonders. They were convinced that God was on their side because of what was going on within their fellowship. They were so certain that 'they had it all' (as indicated by Paul's sarcasm in 1 Corinthians 4:8: 'Already you have all you want! Already you have become rich! Quite apart from us you have become kings!'), that they began to wonder about the authenticity of Paul's ministry. Both letters written to the Corinthians show us that there was much going on in Corinth which covered a variety of aspects of human failure and shortcomings. Paul's answer to the Corinthian church is often made with his tongue in his cheek. This passage about his weakness and the thorn in his flesh helps those concerned with prayer and ministry to the sick to see where the power of God really lies.

The Corinthian church has been boasting about its successes and gifts. Paul talks of his experience of God being made manifest in his weakness. Concentrating on successes, as if by doing so we are proving the existence of God, is the opposite of Paul's understanding of power. We give thanks to God for every person we know who has experienced the healing power of Christ, but we never forget the word of God to Paul: 'My power is made perfect in your weakness'.

3 Holistic health—personal responsibility

Read 1 Corinthians 6:19

The challenge to our attitudes and actions towards our bodies is vital as we consider health and healing. This verse asks us to reflect on how we care for the body. Does our diet contribute to holistic health? In what ways does our lifestyle reflect balance and wholeness? Eating and drinking are important issues, though working and utilizing the strength gained from food is equally important. There is one great purpose for eating—it is to lead to active and fruitful lives (Philippians 1:22).

Without physical well-being or health, one cannot really experience wholeness. If the temple of God, which is the body, is ruined by neglect, there is no possibility of mental, emotional or spiritual well-being. Our natural disability or limitations do not deny wholeness, but wilful neglect and indifference can definitely lead to sickness and ill health.

Part of what is entailed by health involves a concern for the wholeness which is at once physical and mental, spiritual and social. This must begin with caring for the body, which can lead to the well-being of the total person. Fulfilment of the first commandment, to love God, is possible only when we are able to appreciate his gift of life in us, here in the world, and his love for us which is reflected in our physicality. This appreciation is possible only when we feel wholeness in body, soul and spirit. We cannot expect the Holy Spirit to rejoice, living inside a neglected and ruined temple.

4 Holistic health—family responsibility

Read Deuteronomy 6:2–9

While accepting the individual's responsibility for health, it is important to put this into a broader context. Though it is difficult to define precisely what we mean by 'the family', families are an important experience and reality for us all. They need support and encouragement, and the health of this unit will have a significant effect on us all.

One important area is our attitudes. Sometimes parents' attitudes towards one another can determine the attitude towards their children. This can be a chain reaction. Healthy attitudes include loving, caring, understanding, forgiving, appreciating and complimenting one another. Caring is not simply a response to a personal crisis. It is a living and dynamic quality of our lives which needs to be sustained. In this sense parents have a corrective role to perform. Discipline can be redemptive with good counsel, feedback, looking at different options and weighing the consequences. All of these are important in coming to a better and fuller understanding of the role of the family as it helps to promote health and growth and richer development. Good spiritual, emotional and interpersonal relationships make for the trust that belongs with healthy, holistic living.

5 Holistic health—the Church's responsibility

Read Acts 3:1–10

The mission of healing is primarily the mandate given to the Church. A worshipping community is a healing community, which is called upon to bring wholeness to people and the community. In this incident Peter and John represent the Church in action.

In this action we as a Church can learn a number of things.

- ***Wholeness was brought to the lame man who was carried to the temple daily. He represents physical disability, human deprivation and economic exploitation and alienation. The insensitivity of the worshipping community was clear here. The person who needs help lies at the doorstep, ignored by the Church.***

- *Healing took place in the context of worship. Worship is the central source for the mission of the Church. It is the extension of their fellowship.*
- *The man's healing was a team effort. The disciples enter into a relationship of human care and companionship, as demonstrated by Christ while he was on earth.*
- *Their act of healing was not based upon the strength they had, but on what they did not have. Recognizing their emptiness, they discover the real strength.*
- *Their act of healing was one of offering the right kind of fellowship. Extending the right hand symbolized inviting and accepting the other person with dignity and respect. This was done even before the man was healed, when others were reluctant to offer a healing ministry.*

6 Holistic health—community responsibility

Read Mark 2:1–12

This is one of those incidents in the Bible in which the community was involved in bringing health to a person, which in turn brought healing to the community itself. The disease of paralysis not only affects the person but in a way represents the community at large, in that it reveals the inability to fulfil the purpose for which one is called. In other words, when an individual suffers, the community also suffers.

The four people who carried the paralytic man represented the community. They brought him to Jesus, who commended their faith. The faith and belief systems of the community can determine the health of the individual in the community. In this sense, what we believe has an important effect upon our health.

They carried him to the place where Jesus was, not to remove the burden but with a hope that he would be healed. They had to spend their time and wages. It was costly. Here Jesus showed a relationship between sin and sickness. But his emphasis was not on that relationship but his authority to forgive sins. His healing the paralysed man was an act which revealed God. All healing, then, is about revealing the nature of God, whether the community realizes it or not.

The story leaves us with a number of issues to think about. Proper knowledge of health-needs in the community precedes meeting the need. Communication between individuals and families is required. The influences of modernization, urbanization and other dehumanizing forces in society need to be acknowledged and responded to. The forces at work in the community also determine holistic health, which includes the health of the individual and the society. Some health problems can be prevented by having a good social system and social environment. So the role of government and non-government organizations in shaping the community is an important factor in holistic health.

GUIDELINES

Holistic health is the goal of the healing ministry. Health is a gift of God and human efforts are only channels to achieve it. In these Bible studies we have seen the varied responsibilities of different members of the body of our community and society. All are important and all are affected when one is affected. So a healthy co-operation of individuals, families, communities and the Church is necessary to bring wholeness.

In 1 Corinthians 12:4–26, Paul deals with the varieties of spiritual gifts in the Church. Many of the points he makes here can also be applied to the responsibility of bringing holistic health. Healing is the activity of God. Whatever is done towards health contributes to the work of God within his kingdom. Like the various gifts of the Spirit, healing is a 'team ministry' in which each one has their own role to play. Some may be seen more, some are not seen, some are honoured and some are not recognized. But all the 'players' are responsible and important.

In the imagery of the body and its unity, the whole body suffers when one member suffers. Paul highlights three dangers which could also apply to the imagery of health. The first lies in one or another feeling that they have nothing to contribute to the work of bringing holistic health. This can lead to the attitude that health issues are other people's problems, and so we transfer responsibility from ourselves to others. The second danger lies in failing to see the need for the different members of the body to work together. So we do not allow others to exercise their responsibility for health. The third danger comes from thinking that one function is all-important, which leads to ignoring what others have to contribute.

We need an approach that affirms the multiplicity of tasks, functions and gifts. All are responsible and each one has a role to play. The individual cannot ignore his or her responsibility because others are not functioning in the way that they should. This is true for the areas of family, community and Church. We need to work together to bring holistic health.

Further reading

Morris Maddocks, *The Christian Healing Ministry*, SPCK 1990.

James Woodward, *Encountering Illness*, SCM Press 1995.

Denis Duncan, *Health and Healing: A Ministry to Wholeness*, St Andrew Press 1989.

Russ Parker and Roy Lawrence, *Healing and Evangelism*, Triangle 1996.

Nehemiah

When Jerusalem fell to the Babylonians in 587BC, the majority of the rulers and intellectual classes were deported. The books of Ezra and Nehemiah record some of the attempts that were made to return to the land of Israel and rebuild the Jewish nation. The dating of the events described in these two books, and the relation of Ezra and Nehemiah to one another, are uncertain. The books are not simple historical documents, but have been carefully edited in order to emphasize some important themes. The view taken here is that Nehemiah basically records later events than those we find in Ezra. Between them the two books cover about a hundred years, beginning with Cyrus' decree in 538BC and ending with Nehemiah's second term of office in Judea in about 430BC.

The major theme that unites Ezra and Nehemiah is the rebuilding of Jerusalem. In Ezra 1–6 a group of returners rebuild the temple, but work on the walls is stopped (4:21). The arrival of Ezra leads to the equipping and glorification of the temple (7:27). But the city walls are still broken, and this provides the challenge for the first half of Nehemiah (1–7). But this external story is complemented by an internal theme, for the state of the temple and the city reflected the state of the people, who also needed to be rebuilt and rededicated. This is an ongoing challenge, as is emphasized in the second half of Nehemiah (8–13). The editor has carefully shaped the whole, but he has incorporated various historical sources such as lists of people and places. In particular there are first-person 'I/we' accounts that are thought to reflect memoirs by Ezra (Ezra 7–10; Nehemiah 8–10) and Nehemiah (Nehemiah 1–7; 11–13).

In the first week we shall look at the tremendous story portrayed in Nehemiah 1–6, where Nehemiah overcomes all the problems that threaten to prevent the rebuilding of the walls of Jerusalem. In the second week we shall look at the second half of the book, which raises broader issues about the nature of the people of God. The basis for comment will be the New Revised Standard Version (NRSV).

1 A disaster and a prayer *Read Nehemiah 1:1–11*

The first chapter sets out the challenge facing Nehemiah. In the twentieth year of King Artaxerxes I (December 446BC) he hears from his brother Hanani a report about a disastrous event in Jerusalem, perhaps the forced cessation of work on the walls mentioned in Ezra 4:23. Nehemiah's response is the classic psalmic response to trouble—lament.

The prayer here is likely to be the concentrated essence of a time of prayer that lasted no less than four months (see the date of 2:1). The prayer begins, as all prayer must, with an address to God. Nehemiah acknowledges both God's universal power and his gracious covenant relationship with his people. But it is all too evident that Israel has broken the covenant, so that confession follows. The comprehensive character of the prayer means that Nehemiah includes both himself and his family, even though their contribution would have added relatively little to the sum total. Nehemiah knows that God is completely justified in abandoning his people. The only hope lies in God, who has graciously said that exile need not be a full end (cf. Deuteronomy 30:1–5).

A request for God to hear begins the conclusion of the prayer in verse 11a, but 11b springs a surprise. So far the language and prayer has been quite general and based on Israel's traditions of prayer. Suddenly we find a request for success and mercy in the sight of 'this man', the identity of whom is progressively clarified by Nehemiah's final comment and then his naming in 2:1. It is likely that the prayer has been structured to leave this till last and thus provide a transition to the next chapter. With Nehemiah, we trust that God has heard and answered the prayer, and that the next challenge will be one of action. Note that the final plea is not specific. He could have prayed 'Rebuild the walls of Jerusalem' (Psalm 51:18), but Nehemiah simply opens himself to the possibilities of his own situation. Both in structure and content the prayer reveals not only a man of faith but also a planner and doer, with a strategic grasp of the next step and the need to take it at the right time.

2 A crisis and a plan *Read Nehemiah 1:11—2:20*

The initial date corresponds to April 445BC, but far more significant is that it is the beginning of the New Year. Nehemiah probably carefully chose this date to express his sorrow at the state of Jerusalem. There is some evidence that it was customary for kings to be generous at such a time. It was still a dangerous move, for sadness could be mistaken for discontent and kings ensured that discontented people were permanently dealt with. However, Nehemiah has planned carefully and while this does not remove his fear, he is not paralysed. He reassures the king of his loyalty and explains why he is sad. He avoids the dangerous overtones of 'walls' and 'Jerusalem', but highlights his personal grief at the graves and the burnt gates. An encouraging but cautious response by the king is the crucial point at which suspicion may yield to support. At this point Nehemiah prays a quick 'arrow prayer', perhaps 'God of heaven, give me grace before this man.' He then goes on not only to set out his basic plan, but also to make the detailed requests that will ensure its success. No doubt Nehemiah has already penned the letters and will lose no time in getting the king to seal them for sending! He combines a practical realism with a deep trust in a sovereign God.

The action moves forward rapidly and the next section (vv. 9–20) describes Nehemiah's arrival in Jerusalem as governor. But the section is framed at beginning and end by note of the opposition: the powerful and influential Sanballat the Horonite, together with Tobiah the Ammonite. They are later joined by Geshem the Arab (v. 19). They represent the hostility of Jerusalem's neighbours to the establishment of a political and economic rival. Yet this is not all. He has to deal with a broken and demoralized people as well as a broken wall and dangerous enemies. An indication of Nehemiah's awareness of both politics and people is his three-day wait, followed by the secret night-time journey. He knows that leadership needs to be knowledgeable, specific and realistic, as well as inspirational. Above all, leadership depends on God's gracious will. It is Nehemiah's testimony of God's help that provides the key motive in his exhortation to the leaders of the people (v. 18) and enables him to stand firm against opposition (v. 20).

3 A sure defence against the enemy *Read Nehemiah 4:1–23*

Chapter 3 has listed a number of groups rebuilding the walls, reflecting a remarkable feat of organization and, we may safely presume, much active peace-making by Nehemiah. The success leads to opposition that becomes more and more intense throughout the chapter. Whereas previously there had been a brief expression of contempt (2:19), here the enemies join together to mock (v. 2), with the help of a pessimistic jingle (v. 3). This achieves little except a prayer by Nehemiah, and the wall is half completed (v. 6). But although encouraging, this also means that the higher and harder part still remains.

Nehemiah's enemies heighten the tension by plotting physical attack. The response is correspondingly physical—a guard (v. 9), alongside prayer. But this is insufficient, and the fear and uncertainty lower morale and decrease the rate of work (v. 10). Further, the villages that have sent men to help in the rebuilding have no one to protect them and they complain to Nehemiah again and again (v. 12). Nehemiah responds with a radical strategy of defence based on the core family structure, backed up by a reminder of what their God was like. The belief that God frustrates the plans of the wicked and that he fights for his people is at the bedrock of Israelite faith, as witnessed in the book of Exodus.

With the immediate threat dealt with, Nehemiah integrates the defence of the city and the continued building with meticulous care. The reduction in number of those available to work is offset by the rise in morale and the willingness of the people to work from dawn till beyond dusk (v. 21). Although the demands on the people are extreme, they can see the wall going up and know that the duration of the emergency will be limited. A purely defensive strategy would have handed the initiative and possibly the entire war to the opposition.

4 Threat from within *Read Nehemiah 5:1–19*

From external threats we move to internal ones. There was a famine, no doubt made worse by marauding bands of war, and this had so increased the price of grain that many could not afford to live. The safety-net supplied by the law was a system by which loans were given, backed up by a material pledge. However, the situation was so extreme that a number of Jews had been forced to pledge their final resources: their means of livelihood, their houses, and even the service of their children.

Up to this point Nehemiah had dealt strategically with the leaders. Now the people come to him with a bitter complaint. The problem must have been there before the building started, but at last there was a governor who might listen to their complaints. Nehemiah characteristically reflects on the issue (v. 7) before proposing a radical solution appropriate for an extraordinary situation. As in his prayer in chapter 1, he includes himself among those guilty and gives the lead in restoring the pledges taken. It is misleading to translate verse 10 as 'taking of interest', since verse 12 shows that the problem was the 'taking of pledges for debt' (as the REB translates). Nehemiah insists that there be no legal compulsion for the people to give up their possessions when they need to borrow or when loans become due. It is unlikely that this was a complete remission of debts or a permanent measure, and the commitment recorded in 10:31 is more limited. However, it would provide a breathing space during a difficult period.

No doubt Nehemiah's official powers would have enabled him to force the measure through, but those responsible appear to have agreed with Nehemiah (v. 12). Nowadays we tend to be cynical about the motives of leaders, but stories such as this help us gain a vision of a society where the 'fear of our God' (v. 9) has practical political effects. Nehemiah reinforces the verbal assent by exacting an oath. Again, it is rare in the secular West for us to take the role of God seriously in the legal or social realm, but the judgment of God remains the ultimate sanction (vividly expressed by Nehemiah's action in verse 13). But the chapter ends on a positive note. A desire for God's blessing and favour is a powerful incentive for the generous behaviour of godly people like Nehemiah (v. 19).

5 Discretion and valour *Read Nehemiah 6:1–19*

Three final strategies of his enemies are neatly avoided by Nehemiah in this section. General and open threats have achieved nothing, so base assassination becomes the method of last resort. Unlike hapless Gedaliah (Jeremiah 40:13—41:3), Nehemiah is too wise to put himself in the power of his three enemies. Yet neither does he openly accuse them of deceit, for the wall continues to be completed while the conversation continues. The stakes are raised with a direct accusation of treasonable behaviour on the fifth exchange, and we may imagine how sensitive Nehemiah is on this subject. But he does not let it affect the work, answering it with a forthright refutation and another prayer.

The next temptation is even more subtle, for there is a short step between the discretion that Nehemiah has shown towards going outside the city, and cowardly avoidance of any danger by shutting himself in the temple. This could possibly be dressed up as 'prudence' and defended by a statement of how crucial Nehemiah is to the whole project, but Nehemiah has shown himself not to be the sort of leader who avoids danger to his own life. He quickly detects the false note in the concern shown for him, and it may well have been the case that assassination was more likely in the temple than at the walls, surrounded by his supporters. The closing prayer once again commits the betrayal to God's judgment. Nehemiah recognizes that it is impossible for him to exact revenge himself, but that there is a higher court that deals with such treachery. With this assurance he can set aside any bitterness and move on to the next thing.

This next thing is nothing less than the completion of the walls in an amazingly quick time (v. 15). We can be sure that Nehemiah was aware how significant his part had been in the achievement. But he is content to record the amazement of the enemies, and attribute the decisive difference to God's help (v. 16).

6 A city and a people *Read Nehemiah 7:1–7*

In the last few verses of the previous chapter and in these verses we see that Nehemiah has no blind faith in the walls of themselves to protect the people. There remain too many enemies without, and too few defenders within. The unbroken walls are the climax of the main plot of the first half of the book, but Nehemiah is well aware that a city is people before walls, although without walls the city could not flourish in a hostile world.

The first task is to regularize the defence, and the gatekeepers, singers and Levites were probably the best-trained lay police, since their traditional task was to guard the temple. He appoints trustworthy and competent men to be in charge, and arranges for others to be trained as guards. The closing of the doors when the guards are likely to be dozing after their midday meal is another shrewd, temporary measure.

The second, longer-term task, was to ensure that Jerusalem was well-populated by those committed to her welfare and defence (Psalm 122). But who was he to encourage to live there? The solution lay in a list of those who had returned first. The content of the list that follows is basically the same as in Ezra 2, but it is likely that its original place is here.

While the significance placed on birth and lineage may seem to us a prime example of favouritism, we need to remember the context. The story so far has given ample evidence of those who wished to undermine the re-establishment of some sort of Jewish state based on Jerusalem. A good genealogy, and with it a good induction into the traditions and hopes of Israel, could well be the best possible indication of commitment. Indeed, one of the strengths of the Jewish tradition is its sense of continuity with the people of God. Of course, this had its dangers too, as seen in the alternative strands of biblical thought that warn against national pride and emphasize how God wishes to rebuild not just Jerusalem but the entire world (Isaiah 65–66; Luke 3:7–9).

GUIDELINES

Looking back on the story, we can see how Nehemiah overcame one problem after another through his wisdom and his faith. Similar difficulties face the Church today, whose spiritual walls can be as broken as the walls of Jerusalem were. The Church often lacks confidence, and local interests can squash any greater and longer-term vision. Individuals face powerful opposition, perhaps through mockery, sometimes through physical attack. But Nehemiah encourages us to be flexible, faithful and fearless, ready both to pray and act. By meeting one challenge at a time and keeping the overall end in view, he was able to carry the great project through to completion, or at least the end of the beginning. Nehemiah would have appreciated the great prayer of Sir Francis Drake:

O Lord God, when thou givest to thy servants to endeavour any great matter, grant us also to know that it is not the beginning, but the continuing of the same, until it be thoroughly finished, which yieldeth the true glory; through him who for the finishing of thy work laid down his life for us, our Redeemer, Jesus Christ. Amen.

21–27 SEPTEMBER NEHEMIAH 8:1—13:31

1 Reading the law *Read Nehemiah 8:1–18*

This chapter raises some difficult historical and literary questions. The style and content change radically, and Ezra, the hero of the previous era, is the main character. Further, Nehemiah is only mentioned in verse 9, and even then not in some of the ancient versions. One possible solution is to regard 'Nehemiah the governor' to be a textual error, and to regard Nehemiah 8–10 as an editorial insertion referring to an event that took place earlier. This is attractive because there is good reason to raise the issue of the law. Nehemiah may have rebuilt the walls, but the law is the primary means by which the people could be rebuilt.

Whatever the historical background, the chapter reflects a key issue that continues to challenge anyone who reads the Bible. How do we interpret an ancient historical document that refers to times, events and situations that are radically different from those of today? This is particularly urgent if those words come as words from God, whose truth and relevance is proved by Israel's sad story (cf. Nehemiah 1). The first task of Ezra and his Levite helpers was to help the people understand a law that had been forgotten. But the second and greater task was to help the hearers to work out the implications of what they were hearing. It seems to have been the case that the people had understood the law in a way that was too narrow and literalistic. They wept (v. 9) because they realized how impossible it was to keep a law meant for a sovereign Israelite state while they were subject to the Persian authorities.

This was, however, to miss the deeper meaning of the law. The law in the Pentateuch is set within an account of how God saved his people, and it is this note of grace that Ezra asks the people to take to heart. He enables them to recognize that God has been graciously at work in bringing them back to Jerusalem, and the result is a gospel note of joy. Indeed, in essentials the law could be obeyed, as it is in the following account of the celebration of the Festival of Booths. This was the feast at which the exodus was remembered (Leviticus 23:43), and through ritual as well as word the people began to understand how God cared for them and desired for them to flourish. While the concern to do God's will in every detail is commendable, it is always in danger of becoming too earnest and tied to a recognition of failure. When God's grace is primary, then joy and worship are authentic responses.

2 Confessing sins *Read Nehemiah 9:1–8, 32–37*

Again we cannot be sure about the historical setting of this chapter. The Hebrew does not have 'then Ezra blessed the Lord' (v. 6), which could have been a guess by the Greek translators. It could follow on from the previous chapter, but the prayer could also belong elsewhere. It is the content of the prayer that is more important. Here is an opportunity for the gathered people (represented by Levitical leaders) to join in a prayer of confession, similar to that of Nehemiah in chapter 1. It includes an acknowledgment of Israel's sins going right back to the beginning of the nation (so those who were not fully Israelite are not included, v. 2). But it is far more than a statement of sin, for its focus is on God, and this prayer seeks to set Israel's present troubles in the largest possible picture.

The prayer begins with praise to the creator Lord (v. 6). But this same Lord is the one who called Abraham (vv. 7–8) and fulfilled his covenant promises. Alongside an affirmation of God's election of Israel is a recognition that Israel has sinned. The tension between God's purposes and Israel's inclinations is the underlying theme of the review of Israel's history, including the exodus (vv. 9–11), the wilderness period (vv. 12–22), and life in the promised land (vv. 23–31). The overall lesson is one of God's great mercy (v. 31). We could easily add another paragraph that told the gospel story, for there too we find a story of grace, sin, and unlooked-for mercy. God alone is the basis for the element of petition in verse

32. Note how the precise action expected of God is left undefined; it is enough for the problem to be presented to God (cf. Nehemiah 1:11; Matthew 26:39; Romans 8:23).

It is worth reflecting on the character and length of this prayer. Of course, there is a special weight and style appropriate for public and corporate prayer at a key time. Yet it reminds us that biblical prayer characteristically includes praise, confession of sins, and petition. Praise is the first response, with confession its humble complement. Only when both have been fully dealt with is the current state of affairs raised and intercession made. Due recognition of all three dimensions of prayer is an abiding challenge for Christians and churches today.

3 Making an oath *Read Nehemiah 10:28–39*

The confession of sin in the previous chapter leads on naturally to a pledge to keep the law. Once again, it is likely that the ordering is thematic or logical rather than historical, for the details of the stipulations suggest that this followed the events of Nehemiah 13. The way in which the various issues are treated reflects one of the most important developments in post-exilic Judaism. This was a concern to interpret the Pentateuchal law so that it became relevant for a later time. We have already seen Ezra doing that in a general way in chapter 8, and now the people commit themselves to a series of laws that, while not found specifically in the Pentateuch, are logical developments from earlier laws.

So, for example, we find in the Pentateuch an enormous stress on the sabbath and the number seven as the foundation for Israel's worship (e.g. Numbers 28–29). In Nehemiah 13:15–22 we find Nehemiah attempting to reform abuses of the sabbath. Some of these were directly prohibited by the Pentateuchal law, such as performing agricultural work (Exodus 31:14–16). There was no need to repeat that law, because it was clear. But there were other issues that were not covered by the law, such as whether foreigners could sell on the sabbath. Israelite traders could not do this (Amos 8:5), but the issue was raised by the number of non-Israelites mingling with the people. So here the scope of the law is specifically extended to prohibit selling by anyone on the sabbath (v. 31).

Such interpretation and adaptation was essential if the law was not to become a dead letter of merely antiquarian interest. The law is divinely authoritative, but human interpretation is required for it to become relevant to everyday life. Of course, the danger is that the concern for details outweighs the weightier matters of the law, one of the fiercest of Jesus' criticisms of those who inherited the mantle of Ezra and Nehemiah (Matthew 23:23). But it is also true that the New Testament condemns neglect of the economic and social consequences of faith (e.g. James 2). In Nehemiah 8–10 we have a wise balance, where two chapters raise the larger issues (8–9), while this one focuses in on the details. The two approaches (general and particular) will always be in tension, but scripture insists on keeping them close together.

4 Dedicating the wall *Read Nehemiah 12:27–47*

We return to the first person account of Nehemiah himself. We left him in chapter 7 with the wall complete, but there is one final stage to go—its dedication. As we would expect, the impressive and all-inclusive ceremony is organized to perfection, yet with the glory of God clearly in view. The Levites and the people are divided into two great companies, both of which include choir, prominent layman, lay leaders, priests, director of music and Levitical musicians. Nehemiah could easily have made himself leader of a unified procession. But the division of the company not only adds richness and diversity to the ceremony, but also emphasizes how he is a servant of the people. The key note is of thanksgiving (v. 31) and praise, represented by the musical instruments (vv. 27, 35). It is likely that Israel's choir was often divided into two for antiphonal singing. Here, Nehemiah has transposed into a geographical key the praise of the God who founded, sustained and rebuilt Jerusalem. The logic of the liturgical movement is a move from circle to centre. At its climax both groups meet harmoniously at the house of God (v. 40).

The ceremony succeeds in integrating and summing up the key building achievements of both books of Ezra and Nehemiah. When the worship of Jerusalem had been re-established, the sound was heard far away, but it was a mixture of joy and weeping (Ezra 3:13). The same mixture was found at the reading of the law

(Nehemiah 8:9, 12, 17). The dedication of the temple, described in Ezra 6:13–18, allowed sacrifices to be offered again in the proper way. Yet without the walls the city and its temple and the God to whom it was dedicated are open to attack, defilement and mockery. Now the walls are built and the motifs of previous high points are taken up and carried further—walls, temple, sacrifices, a sound that could be heard far away, and above all unalloyed joy. There is a time for mourning, but there is also a time for rejoicing, and the wholehearted celebration of the achievement of a great work needs no apology. Verse 43 sounds the note of joy no less than five times. Although such times will be rare, they are proper reminders for Christians that God has been at work building an even greater city, where joy will finally triumph over mourning (Revelation 21).

5 Sustaining the temple service *Read Nehemiah 12:44—13:14*

Nehemiah 13:6–7 alerts us to a time gap between 12:43 and 12:44, despite the repetition of 'on that day'. It is likely that here again the editor has made a point rather than told us what happened in strict chronological order. Grand ceremonies organized from on high are of little use if they do not reflect and further a commitment by the whole people. The comments at the end of chapter 12 emphasize that the necessary means to support the temple and its service were joyfully given by the people. The mention of David and Asaph (v. 46) hints that the spirit of the worship as well as its form was worthy of that golden age.

However, reform is often a superficial and unwanted upheaval. Nehemiah's absence after his stint as governor allowed his arch-enemy Tobiah to set up in Jerusalem. On his return he angrily throws Tobiah's furniture out of his rooms. There was no doubt a personal element in this reaction, but the cleansing and return of the temple vessels (13:9) suggest that the holiness of God and his house was Nehemiah's chief concern. This is also at the root of his rebuke of the officials who have neglected the maintenance of the temple and its servants (vv. 10–11).

Christians can sometimes think that the Old Testament interest in the temple and its service is a lighter matter in comparison with issues of justice and forgiveness. But we would do well to remember that at the climax of Jesus' ministry was a similar attack on the temple furniture (Mark 11:15). The temple was, for good or for ill, at the heart of a web of relations, economic, social, political and religious. When we seek to evaluate the fierce arguments that the reordering of a church and its worship occasions today, it is perhaps worth remembering that both for Nehemiah and Jesus the primary motives were the honour of God and a concern for the powerless.

6 Mixed days and mixed marriages *Read Nehemiah 13:15–31*

The two paragraphs in this section (beginning at v. 15 and v. 23) show the same pattern. Nehemiah sees an abuse, takes steps to deal with it, argues forcibly with those responsible, and copes with related matters. It may appear to those brought up in a modern pluralist society that much is being made of nothing much. Sunday trading is now a common practice, and Christians often join in. Then, with values absorbed from countless romantic stories, we are hurt by Nehemiah's disregard for the feelings of the young men and women he curses and beats.

However, the very vehemence of Nehemiah's action forces us to reflect on the very different assumptions that underlay his action. In the modern West, tolerance and trade are primary values. The majority would simply not understand, let alone put first, ideas such as the holiness of the Lord's day or the distinctiveness of God's people. But for Nehemiah it is of the utmost concern that there is no contamination of the people of God by those with different beliefs and values. Nehemiah appeals to the hard lessons that God taught his people in their past history. Breaking the sabbath had led to the destruction of Jerusalem (see Jeremiah 17:21–27). Even if it was selling rather than buying that was specifically forbidden, the collusion of Jew and Gentile clearly broke the spirit if not the letter of the law. As for the problem of mixed marriages, Nehemiah draws a comparison with Solomon, whose political marriages led him to sin and apostasy, and ultimately to the split of the kingdom.

Although Nehemiah is uncompromising and definitely undemocratic, it is hard to see how Jewish identity could have been sustained without such measures. The birth of the nation was an integrated political, social and religious event, and assimilation to the surrounding culture would have destroyed the basis of its identity. The issue is more complex for the Church, for it is no longer bound by geographical, racial or cultural ties. Yet time and again church historians have shown how churches have allowed themselves to be wedded to the spirit and culture of the age, and have disappeared. Indeed, in many parts of the West this has nearly happened. Does Nehemiah have something special to teach us at such a time?

GUIDELINES

The triumphant story of the first half of the book has given way to a much more ambiguous and complex account of Israel's life. Material and financial difficulties often appear to hinder the work of the Church, but rebuilding the physical walls is the simpler part of Nehemiah's task. The greater challenge is how to deal with the sins and weaknesses of God's people. Nor has the coming of Christ and the gift of the Holy Spirit eliminated those challenges. The Church still needs strong leaders, a firm grasp of God's word, and a willingness to engage with attacks on its self-identity, whether from a cultural, economic or religious point of view.

Most gracious Father,
we pray for your holy catholic Church:
fill it with all truth, and in all truth with all peace;
where it is corrupt, purge it;
where it is in error, direct it;
where anything is amiss, reform it;
where it is right, strengthen and confirm it;
where it is in want, furnish it;
where it is divided, heal it and unite it in your love;
through Jesus Christ our Lord. Amen.

After a prayer by Archbishop William Laud

Further reading

D. Kidner, *Ezra and Nehemiah: Tyndale Commentary*, IVP 1979.

H.G.M. Williamson, *Ezra, Nehemiah: Word Biblical Commentary*, Word 1985.

The Parable of Lazarus and the Rich Man

For two weeks we will be reflecting on the parable of Lazarus and the rich man in Luke 16:19–31, a parable that is often ignored. This may be due to an uneasiness with what the parable appears to be saying. The passage is frequently seen as a 'reversal of roles'. On first reading, the story seems to be saying, 'Life is unfair. But, never mind, God will "even things up" in the next life. Lazarus had a hard time here—and thus enjoyed good times in heaven. The rich man had a good life on earth, so he ends up in hell.' Put bluntly, the parable would then mean, 'If you are comfortable here, hell awaits you. If you are homeless here, heaven is guaranteed to you.' Indeed, there *are* stories like this in both Greek and Jewish literature from the time of Jesus, but does Jesus endorse them? Surely not.

How then are we to view this parable? In the next fortnight we will attempt an answer. But before beginning, a word about method may be helpful. In the late nineteenth century a famous German New Testament scholar, Adolf Julicher, ably discredited the irresponsible allegorization of the parables. For centuries, interpreters did things like identifying the innkeeper in the parable of the good Samaritan as the apostle Paul and seeing Jesus in the fatted calf of the parable of the prodigal son. Julicher felt that the only way to get rid of such nonsense was to insist that each parable had only *one* theme. Now, a hundred years later, we can both honour his goal and move beyond his suggested method of achieving it.

It is impossible to accept the idea that the parable of the prodigal son has only a single theme. The story is too comprehensive. Furthermore, conceptual theological statements deal with clusters of themes. Does John 3:16 have *one* theme? God, love, world, giving, son, only begotten, believe, perish, eternal life—all of these appear *together*. If this is true for conceptual theological statements, what about parables? Why must they be limited to a single theme?

The story of Lazarus and the rich man contains many themes skilfully woven together. Our task is to see which ideas were placed in the story by Jesus for his audience. In so doing we discover what Jesus is saying to all of us.

28 SEPTEMBER–4 OCTOBER

1 God and mammon: Lazarus and the rich man

Read Luke 16:9–13

A few verses before the parable of Lazarus, Jesus presents a short poem on God and mammon. The poem can be understood as an introduction to the parable. Mammon is an Aramaic word that means 'material possessions' or 'money'. This short poem says three things about mammon relevant to the parable.

First, Jesus says, 'You cannot serve two masters ... you cannot serve God and mammon.' The problem with material possessions is that they take on the characteristics of a personified force that seeks to master us. Yes, they are necessary to sustain life and they can be used to serve God. But the danger is always there. The pressure never lessens. This is why possessions are called 'unrighteous mammon'. Mammon seeks to usurp God and take over our lives. Jesus warns us that we cannot serve both God and mammon. We must choose between them.

Secondly, Jesus asks the question: if you have not been faithful with mammon, who will entrust the truth to you? There is a play on words here in Aramaic, which was the language Jesus spoke at home. He is saying, 'If you have not been *amin* (faithful) in the unrighteous mammon, the *amuna* (the truth) who will *ja'min ith kun* (entrust to you)?' The root AMN, from which we have the word 'Amen', is used four times. The point is clear: if we cheat on our taxes we will never understand the gospel. If I have not been faithful before God with material things, how can I expect God to give me an even greater treasure (his truth)?

Jesus' third point reinforces the second. He concludes by saying, 'If you have not been faithful in what is another's, who will give to you what is your own?' All our possessions belong to God because 'the earth is the Lord's and the fulness thereof'. This basic biblical principle is foreign to the contemporary capitalist West. The pen in my pocket, the watch on my wrist, the computer with which I type these reflections—all belong to God. I am only a steward of them. They are not mine. This includes the car I drive, the house in which we live and the garden behind our house. They are not mine. My government thinks they are, so I am obliged to pay taxes, but I know better—they belong to God and one day I will be held accountable for what I have done with them. So if all my possessions belong to God, is there anything that is *really* mine? Yes. That small part of the truth of God which I have managed to understand and live out is truly mine and I will 'take it with me'. God looks to see if I am a faithful steward of material things. If I demonstrate faithfulness, God then reveals the gospel to me. What I grasp of it is *really* mine. A restoration of this world-view could transform our societies and our lives.

With this in place as a foundation, Jesus appears to be saying, 'Now, I will tell you a story of two people. One served God and the other mammon.' So we are prepared for the story of Lazarus.

2 Who is El-'Azar (Lazarus)? *Read Luke 16:19–31*

This parable is the third of a trilogy. In the first, a *prodigal* wastes his *father's* possessions (Luke 15:11–32). In the second, a dishonest *steward* wastes his *master's* possessions (16:1–8). Here in the third, a *master* wastes his *own* possessions. All three, properly understood, deal with the theme of salvation.

The parable of Lazarus and the rich man opens with a brief yet brilliant picture of a self-indulgent rich man who cares for nothing and no one but himself. We are then told of a sick, hungry, neglected, poor beggar lying in the street outside his gate. We will focus on the rich man later. Initially we must ask about the poor man's name. Why a name, and why *this* name? Lazarus is the only person named in all of the parables of Jesus. It must be deliberate. In Hebrew 'Lazarus' means 'the one whom God helps'. There he lay, day after day at the rich man's gate, and received nothing. He was so sick he could not stand, and so poor he was reduced to begging. Did God really help him?

I was a professor in a theological college in Beirut, Lebanon, for ten years during the recent Lebanese civil war. A blind beggar stood at the gate of the Greek Orthodox church near the college. He was a quiet, gentle man with a lovely face. He did not cry out in the traditional fashion of beggars. He had a wooden box strapped to his shoulder and waist, with a hinged glass top full of chewing gum. He was a 'shopkeeper'. I bought Chicklets whenever I saw him, paid him double and then gave the gum to street children in the next block. He and I became friends. The war around us triggered horrible passions, but not in this man. His quiet calm was never broken, regardless of the cannon fire in the distance or the rattle of machine-guns a street away. An inner peace radiated from him to all those around him. His name was 'Abd al-Rahman' (the servant of the Compassionate One). The Compassionate One naturally shows compassion. Did God show compassion to him? He was a blind beggar! How could he be so at peace? The rest of us did not manage this.

The rich man in the parable neglected and thus despised beggars. But in the end he became one. In hell he cried out, 'Have mercy on me' (the traditional cry of a Middle Eastern beggar). These exact words were spoken by the blind beggar outside Jericho (Luke 18:38). The rich man then asked for divine help via Abraham. He wanted to become El-'Azar (Lazarus), the one whom God helps. But the arrogant complainer, the demander of services, was not and could not become El-'Azar.

Yes, God helped Lazarus. As we continue our study we will witness a Lazarus who maintained dignity, gentleness, kindness, and long-suffering patience as he lay week after week uncared for, outside the rich man's gate. Are such actions and attitudes really possible without divine help? So today, where can we find Lazarus, the one whom God helps? Look for the loving, forgiving spirit in the midst of pain and you will have found him. Your search may take you to a cross. And can we become like him?

3 Lazarus and the question: what now?

Review Luke 16:19–31; read Mark 8:34–38

Lazarus is the Job of the New Testament. The book of Job is a great biblical treasure not because of what happens to Job, but because of the way in which he responds. Job's wife calls on him to curse

God and die. He refuses. Instead he says, 'The Lord gave and the Lord hath taken away, blessed be the name of the Lord.' In the middle of his trials he cries out, 'Though he slay me, yet will I trust in him.' At the end he is not given an answer to the question of why he suffers. Instead God walks on to the stage and Job's question evaporates. He concludes, 'I have spoken once ... but I will proceed no further.' We, the readers, observe his response to what happens to him. By his response Job creates meaning for himself and for all of us.

The Bible never really answers the question, 'Why do the righteous suffer?' Life was not fair to Job and he says so. Our parable does not tell us why Lazarus had a hard life. Look carefully: Abraham in Luke 16:25 does not make a 'tit-for-tat' connection. Rather, he simply affirms that Lazarus *received* evil things in his earthly life. What evil things? The real evil that he endured was neither poverty nor illness, but the daily indifference of the rich man. The rich man gave Lazarus evil things by ignoring him. The priest did the same to the wounded man beside the road in the parable of the good Samaritan. Like the wounded man, Lazarus was in bad shape.

Lazarus was among the poorest of the poor. Thus he was a beggar. He was also too sick to walk. He 'was laid' each day outside the rich man's gate. The verb in Greek is a passive, and Arabic and Syriac translations in the Middle East have always preserved that passive. Each day Lazarus' friends carried him to the street outside the rich man's gate. People in the community respected him and helped him the only way they could. They carried him to 'work' each day and took him home each night. The rich man did not feed him, so his friends must have done so. He was loved and respected.

For his part, Lazarus did not turn bitter or vengeful. He did not stone the dogs around him, out of the anger and frustration of his existence. When the rich man started to suffer he immediately began complaining. Lazarus was quiet. Patience and long-suffering were his responses to privation, disease and neglect. Surely this is at the heart of why the community cared for him.

When, and after, hard times fall on us, the question is not 'why?' but rather 'what now?' Both Job and Lazarus chose to create meaning out of the depths. Is this a part of what Jesus meant when he said, 'Take up your cross and follow me'?

4 Lazarus and the dogs

Review Luke 16:19–31; read Mark 1:9–13

Lazarus lay each day amidst the heat and flies of the village street. The dogs gathered and licked his sores. Many commentators think that the dogs are a part of his torment. I am very sure such an understanding is not intended. Dogs in the Middle East are not pets. In the early Jewish tradition, dogs were considered almost as unclean as pigs. When the Samaritans, in anger, wanted deliberately to defile the Jewish temple, they entered the temple complex secretly on the eve of Passover and spread the bones of dogs across the courts. The temple was thus defiled and the Jews could not celebrate the Passover.

The dogs in our story may be wild street scavengers. But there is another possibility. They may be guard dogs kept by the rich man to protect his property. Such dogs would naturally eat 'what fell from the rich man's table'. In the parable we find Lazarus *longing* to be fed those scraps. But they are thrown to the semi-wild guard dogs that no one dares approach save their master. No one? Not quite! Lazarus manages to make friends with the wild dogs, be they street scavengers or (more likely) guard dogs. They know that this kindly man is their friend. How do they respond to Lazarus?

The saliva of a dog's mouth is sterile because it is always moving. The ancients of the Middle East discovered that wounds and sores would heal more quickly if they were licked by a dog. In pre-Christian times centres were established where people could be taken to have their sores or wounds licked by trained dogs. In Israel archaeologists have recently discovered a huge canine burial ground for such dogs, dating from about 400BC, in Aschalon on the Mediterranean.

The dogs in this parable are not trained dogs, yet they know how to help their friend. The Greek text contains the critical word *alla* (but) in Luke 16:21. The rich man would not give Lazarus anything, not even the scraps from his sumptuous banquets, '*but* the dogs came and licked his sores'. That is, the people would not help him but the dogs tried to make up for them!

From this beautiful scene we discover a great deal about the person of Lazarus. He was kind and gentle. He lived in quiet harmony with the animal world around him, regardless of the harshness of his environment. Many of the Desert Fathers exhibited the same harmony with wild animals. We recall Jerome and the lion in the region of Bethlehem. A lion was terrorizing the neighbourhood. Jerome went out into the wilderness, made friends with the lion and pulled a large thorn from its paw. The lion became his friend and is usually pictured curled up at his feet. We remember St Francis and the wolf. Friendly lions attended the funeral of Paul the Hermit. St Cuthbert of England was saved from the incoming tide by sea-lions. The list goes on and on, and notably begins with Jesus in the wilderness who 'was with the wild beasts' (Mark 1:13).

With the briefest of strokes Jesus has painted a clear picture of Lazarus' soul. He is a man at peace with himself—within his suffering—and is thus in harmony with the natural world around him. Does he sense that the dogs, like himself, are unjustly despised and ill-treated and thus transformed into angry wild animals? We are not told. But there is much to ponder here.

Do we, in our pain, live in peace with all God's creatures around us? Let us pray for this peace that also passes understanding.

5 Lazarus responds to verbal abuse in the next life

Review Luke 16:19–31; read Luke 6:32–36

We have noted how in this life Lazarus responded to privation, illness and cruel neglect. Now we will examine his response to abuse in life after death.

At death Lazarus was too poor for a funeral. But Abraham and the angels throw a party to welcome him. To recline 'in the bosom of Abraham' meant lying on a U-shaped couch called a 'triclinium' in the place of honour to the right of Abraham. At the Last Supper, the beloved disciple reclined 'in/on the bosom of Jesus' (John 13:23). Such is the place reserved for Lazarus beside Abraham. In his earthly life the rich man enjoyed sumptuous banquets every day. Now we read of a banquet for Lazarus.

The rich man observes this scene from hell. He recognizes Lazarus and knows his name. So the rich man *did* realize that this beggar was at his gate, and he knew his name! Yet he showed Lazarus no mercy! Surely now, cast into hell, seeing Lazarus honoured by Abraham, the rich man will apologize to him and request his forgiveness. Amazingly, this is not the case. We are shocked to hear the rich man demanding services from Lazarus.

Those who are listening to the parable are electrified! The tables are turned! Lazarus is in a position of power, reclining beside a man of great influence—no less than Abraham himself! How will Lazarus respond now to being treated as a servant and asked to serve a man who consistently ignored his suffering? We expect him to explode in rage and say something like, 'You half dead dog! I see you recognize my face and can call my name! You saw me outside your gate, but you did nothing to alleviate my pain. Your dogs were kind to me. They licked my wounds. But you—you no-good scum of the earth—where were you when I needed your help? Now you want *me* to serve *you*?! I can't believe it! Abraham, leave this rubbish to fry in hell until the flesh falls off his bones. He fed his dogs! He would not feed me. What he's suffering is only half of what he deserves.'

But no. Lazarus is quiet. This gentle, long-suffering man has no stored-up anger ready to explode, no reflections of retaliation in the waking hours of the night, no score to settle, no vengeance to exact. Like Job, he creates meaning for all of us by his response to what happens to him. Lazarus is a model of the mercy of his heavenly Father, described in Luke 6:35–36.

We have seen this before—on Golgotha.

6 Mission at our doorstep

Review Luke 16:19–31; read James 2:14–17

In traditional Middle Eastern village life, beggars naturally congregate in the places where there is the greatest possibility of a handout. Often a cluster of beggars is found outside the church on Sunday mornings. They hope that the worshippers' hearts will have been quickened to care for the poor during the service. Lying outside a rich man's gate is a part of the same psychology. The rich man is the only person in town with an abundance of food. Lazarus lies outside the rich man's gate each day in hope that he might be fed. Having faced the 'beggars' gauntlet' on numerous occasions for decades in the Middle East, I know something of the dynamics of the scene. It is easy to survive by developing 'compassion fatigue'. Beggars are ever present. There are so many of them. One's resources are limited—finally one just doesn't notice them any more. Compassion fatigue becomes a way to cope, a way to survive.

The person who works in a bakery cannot smell the fresh bread and the clerk in a chocolate shop cannot smell the chocolate. Even so with the pain of others—we become immune to it and are no longer shocked by it. Like famine in Africa—we call it 'traditional famine' and go on with life. At times it is easier to be concerned about the homeless in Bosnia than to try to do something about those sleeping rough in our own towns. Far away, someone else has to get their hands dirty and deal with the mess. But what of the kids sleeping in the Tube station? It's better not to notice them. And besides, what can anyone do anyway? Isn't it a government problem?

Mission must always involve both the brother and sister far away as well as the needy near at hand. One of my favourite hymns says:

> ***I bind my heart this day***
> ***to the brother far away***
> ***and the brother near at hand***
> ***in this town and in this land***

The rich man saw Lazarus with his eyes but never his heart. Yet when he needed Lazarus he found a voice to call his name. James has a few things to say about those who see the hungry and intone, 'Go in peace, be warmed and filled' (2:16). Perhaps this is one of those cases where the parables of Jesus shine through the pages of the book of James.

May we pledge ourselves afresh to *see* the Lazaruses at our doorsteps even as we continue to be concerned for brothers and sisters far away.

In a book of recollections of Anne Frank by her friends, the most telling were from those who knew her after she was arrested and sent to Nazi concentration camps. One story stuck in my mind. A woman with whom Anne was imprisoned in the final camp before her death said of her, 'She was the only one whose tears never ran dry.' Others survived the daily horrors by no longer seeing or feeling. Not so Anne Frank.

The rich man saw Lazarus with his eyes, but had no feeling for him.

5–11 OCTOBER

1 False formulae *Review Luke 16:19–31; read John 9:1–7*

The parable of Lazarus and the rich man flatly denies two false formulae. The first of these is, 'If you have suffered, you must be a sinner.' Granted, if you 'do' drugs and 'fry' your brains you will destroy yourself. Any self-destructive lifestyle will eventually result in disintegration and suffering. Yes, sin can lead to suffering. But the formula cannot be reversed. When we see a person suffering we cannot automatically say, 'It is because he or she has sinned.' The book of Job speaks to this problem. Job was an upright and righteous man and he endured unspeakable suffering.

Actually the book of Job really focuses on a related question: 'Does Job serve God for naught?' The answer is a clear and unqualified 'yes'. Job maintains his faith and integrity throughout the pain and loss he endures. The same is true of Lazarus. In this life and in the next he appears humbly as a friend of animals, people, the angels and Abraham, the father of us all. There is no hint in the parable that Lazarus suffered because of any evil for which he was responsible. Besides, much of his suffering could be traced to evil in the life of the rich man.

The formula 'sin = suffering' persisted into New Testament times. When faced with a man born blind Jesus is asked, 'Did this man sin or his parents that he was born blind?' Amazingly this attitude persisted despite the book of Job. In the modern world we are inflicted with a much milder form of the same mental attitude. We may not endorse the crude formula: 'suffering = sin'. Yet it is easy for those with jobs to dismiss the jobless with oversimplifications such as, 'They can't find work because they are lazy or have not worked hard enough to become qualified.' In short: they are suffering because they have sinned. Sometimes that may be the case. But as a formula it is a tragic perversion.

A second sub-Christian formula seems to emerge in every age, namely, 'If you are a true Christian you will end up wealthy.' If you control your appetites and live a disciplined life you may be able to save money and get ahead financially. But Lazarus is a gentle, forgiving man and he is poor. The rich man is a self-indulgent, self-centred monster and yet he is wealthy.

Jesus' masterful parable clears the theological air of these false formulae. We are challenged to reflect on traces of them that continue to afflict our society and our lives.

2 Repentance and the parable of Lazarus

Review Luke 16:19–31; read Isaiah 55:6–9

The root meaning of repentance is *return*. In the Old Testament, this can be a return to God or a return to the land. In the New Testament, repentance/return is always a return to God, never a return to the land. What then does this parable say about repentance as a return to God? Two things come into focus.

First, it is clear that there is no chance for a 'return to God' after death. The rich man is told that a great chasm has been fixed between the house of Abraham and the rich man's abode and 'those who would go from there to here cannot'. The rich man appears to understand this. He wants Lazarus to return to the earth and warn his brothers 'lest they come to this place of torment'. The issue would not be pressing if the rich man could tell his brothers on arrival to look elsewhere. But if their decision to separate from God is a final decision then the issues are critical. The rich man seems to be aware of this.

Scripture is consistently clear on this point. When Isaiah 55:6 urges his readers to 'seek the Lord while he may be found; call upon him while he is near', he implies that God will not always be found and he will not always be near. When we contemplate these awesome thoughts, we naturally long for the possibility of a return to God remaining open after death. Would not a loving God want it so?

C.S. Lewis's novel *The Great Divorce* deals brilliantly with this issue. In that imaginative tale a busload of people from hell take a trip to heaven. On arrival they quickly find it unbearable. The residents of heaven do their utmost to persuade them to remain. But one after another they board the bus to return to their isolated lives and homes in hell.

Eternal separation from God is not a harsh judgment hurled down upon innocent unbelievers from on high. Rather, it is a free choice that we make ourselves. How we live our lives on this earth is related to that choice. The rich man used his resources for self-indulgent excesses. He feasted sumptuously every day. That meant that he did not keep the sabbath and did not allow his staff to keep it. In short, he cared nothing about them or about keeping God's law, let alone for the neighbour outside his gate. This parable pointedly illustrates that the rich man was obliged to take responsibility for his choice. Let us take seriously our responsibility to love God and our neighbour.

3 Wealth, social responsibility and Lazarus

Review Luke 16:19–31; read Luke 12:13–21

The parable of Lazarus clearly affirms that the rich man failed in his responsibilities to the needy man at his gate. The rich man had more than enough. His half-eaten meals were thrown to his dogs. Lazarus longed to eat those scraps but they were not given to him. God was pleased with Lazarus' quiet, patient endurance, but not with the rich man's social irresponsibility. Wealth, be it little or much, is not condemned in scripture. What is criticized is the failure to see that all we own belongs to God. We are merely stewards of God's treasures. Furthermore, the rich man is a fine example of a person whose wealth became his master. Having failed to acknowledge God as his master, he soon came under the sway of mammon. He has a large staff. There are sumptuous banquets every day. What does he have them do? Serve him—nothing else! He does not keep the law. His staff are not granted a weekly day of rest.

He is also dressed 'in purple'. Purple was so expensive that only the very wealthy could afford it. As well, the rich man wore 'fine linen'. The word in Greek is *bussos*, a transliteration of the Hebrew *butz* which meant 'Egyptian cotton'. This was often used for underclothes. There may be a note of humour here: the rich man had very expensive robes; he also had high-quality undergarments!

The parable of the rich fool is further commentary on the same theme. In it a bumper crop assures a rich landowner of even greater surpluses. He thinks of no one beyond himself and earns the succinct judgment, 'Thou fool!' from God. The story of Ananias and Sapphira in Acts 5 illustrates that the New Testament is not against private property. These two early believers were free to do what they wished with what they owned. They were condemned because they lied to the apostles. Paul tells his readers to work so that they can support themselves and be able to help those in need (see 1 Thessalonians 4:11f). Both of these goals are noble and involve us in the acquisition and use of material resources. The question, however, remains: who is the master—God or mammon? For the rich man, the answer was 'mammon'. When mammon becomes a master it corrupts our view of ourselves and makes us blind to the needy around us.

'O Lord our God, thee and thee only would I serve.'

4 Pride of race and Abraham

Review Luke 16:19–31; read Luke 3:7–9

In his speech from hell the rich man saw and recognized Abraham. He then called Abraham by name. The Greek text, appropriately translated into English, reads 'Father Abraham'. However, the Syriac translations from the second to the seventh centuries and the Arabic translations from the eighth century to the present day have translated without exception, '*my* Father Abraham'. This has to do with idiom. In Aramaic it is quite impossible to say 'Father Abraham'. Idiomatic speech necessitates 'my Father Abraham'. In the same manner, young boys were never addressed as 'son' but as 'my son', and the village priest was never simply called 'father' but always 'our father'. I am confident that the personal pronoun is implied in the Greek text even if it doesn't appear.

In any case, the rich man saw himself as a member of the family of Abraham and obviously expected Abraham to help him. The blood of Abraham ran in his veins. Did that not grant him automatic status and privilege? Racism takes many forms. The rich man was infected by one of them. If anyone could claim privilege on the basis of racial connection, surely it was a son of Abraham!

John the Baptist was faced with the same attitude. He cried out, 'Do not begin to say to yourselves, "We have Abraham as our father": for I tell you, God is able from these stones to raise up children to Abraham' (Luke 3:8). The issue was repentance and the fruit worthy of it. Having the blood of Abraham in their veins was irrelevant. Jesus agreed. In this parable the rich man lived his self-centred life and ignored the needy around him. In the final analysis his racial connection to Abraham guaranteed him nothing.

This point was clearly important to Jesus. He could have had the story conclude with a conversation between the rich man and the angel Gabriel. After all, the angels carried Lazarus to heaven. So why not have the rich man talk to an angel? Instead Jesus introduces the figure of Abraham. The point is obvious. The rich man's racial ties to Abraham neither protect him from hell nor guarantee heaven. The rich man's commitments and lifestyle were what mattered. In the process all forms of racism are vigorously opposed.

But there is a second aspect to Abraham's presence. Abraham was a man of faith who went forth not knowing where he was going. He left his country, his father's house and his gods in costly obedience to the one true God who spoke to him. So is the rich man really a son of Abraham? Did he pay a price for his obedience to the God of Abraham? The story denies the value of any racial claim to merit. It also challenges us to reflect on the commitments we make when we call Abraham our father.

5 Theodicy: is God just?

Review Luke 16:19–31; read Micah 6:3–8

As noted, many commentators have seen this parable as an attempt to answer the question of God's justice. A rich man has more than enough. A poor man is sick and hungry. Where is the justice of God? Answer: in the next life, when the rich man had it tough and God compensated the poor man by giving him good things. We have seen the inadequacy of this understanding of the text. Yet the parable does say something about the justice of God. So how does Jesus understand God's justice?

Abraham calls on the rich man to *remember*. This is a classical biblical cry. In Micah God calls out, 'My people, remember … that you may know the saving acts of the Lord.' The call to recollection is a serious call. The rich man is called upon to remember four things:

- ***You received your good things (his extravagant life)***
- ***Lazarus received only bad things (his sickness and hunger)***
- ***Lazarus is comforted (in Abraham's bosom)***
- ***You are in anguish (in hell)***

These four statements exactly match the four scenes in the parable itself. They are even in the same order. English translations often put the word 'but' before the third statement. Yet it is not there in the Greek text. We should read '*and* he is comforted' rather than '*but* he is comforted'. The point is not *contrast* but *continuity*. Abraham is saying to him, 'You (rich man) received (passive) many material possessions. Remember—reflect on what you had and what you did with it! You "wasted your life in expensive living", you prodigal! Give an account of your stewardship, you unjust steward! Lazarus received evil—from you!! Remember, rich man—remember! You responded with self-indulgence and indifference while he responded with patience and gentleness. So we honour him for his choices! As for you—you have your just reward!'

The question of the origin of evil is not addressed. God is not blamed for Lazarus' illness. We do not know what caused it, but we do know that Lazarus also suffered from heat, flies, dust and hunger—all of which could have been prevented by the rich man. In addition to this was an inevitable sense of worthlessness that added to his pain. The message is, 'He received evil things *from you*.' At the end of the story we feel that God is just. Each received what his own commitments and actions justly deserved.

We are left with a paradox. Yes, life is unfair—yet God is just.

6 Miracle and faith *Review Luke 16:19–31; read John 11:45–53*

The rich man pleads for Lazarus to return to earth and warn his brothers. He thinks that if only someone from the dead goes to them they will repent. Abraham does not agree. Nor does Jesus. Why not? We recall that another man named Lazarus did rise from the dead (John 11:38–44). The result was that Jesus' opponents were all the more determined to get rid of him. Furthermore, the rich man saw Lazarus reclining at a banquet beside Abraham. That is, the rich man received the witness of one who arose from the dead. Yet that rich man expressed no remorse and evidenced no change of attitude towards Lazarus. In his customary self-centred way he only demanded services. So why does the rich man think that things will be any different with his brothers?

Repentance and faith come to us in mysterious ways. Undeniable historical proof is not one of them. Paul says, 'Faith comes from what is heard, and what is heard comes by the preaching of Christ' (Romans 10:17). Through proclamation in the act of worship, faith is born through a mysterious working of the Spirit of God in the believer's heart. But there is more.

Faith in the New Testament is defined in three ways. It is intellectual assent, a daily walk of trust and a response of obedience. Different texts assume or teach different aspects of this great mystery. As they come together, living faith is born. Living faith operates in a different realm from the world of historical facts. I know my family loves me. I have a great deal of evidence for this. But what if I were constantly demanding proof? Tragically, I would always be asking for evidence and the evidence would never be enough. Mathematics lends itself to proof. The deep realities that sustain life and make it meaningful cannot be reduced to verifiable history or mathematical formula. I believe I am the son of Ewing Bailey and Annette Meader Bailey. I believe I am the father of two children. I believe the Word has become flesh and dwelt among us. I have never sought objective scientific proof of any of these truths which lie at the heart of who I am.

To try to prove that God exists beyond any shadow of doubt is a misunderstanding of the nature of the truth we seek. The wind blows and we see its effect but do not know where it comes from or where it goes. At the end of the day we recall Paul's affirmation that faith is a gift of the Holy Spirit (Romans 8:15–17; 1 Corinthians 12:9).

Come, Holy Spirit—bear witness with our spirits that we are indeed children of God!

GUIDELINES

Once we see Jesus as a skilled metaphorical theologian in the rabbinic tradition, we begin to look for theological richness in his teachings. In this great parable we are not disappointed. Rather, we are almost embarrassed by a wealth of treasures.

Of the many themes that present themselves to us here, which stands out from the others as a central teaching of the parable? Each of us must give our own answer and these will vary, depending on who we are and where we are in our pilgrimages to the city of God. For me, the pivotal focus of the story is found where we see Lazarus, the one whom God helps, as a New Testament Job. Like Job, Lazarus creates meaning by his quiet, long-suffering, patient response to the tragedy of his life, his sickness and neglect. What dreams were dashed and what hopes of his family were shattered as he descended through illness, and who knows what else, to the dusty road outside the rich man's house? The care of the community and the compassion of the dogs eloquently define the heroics of his response. His silence before the rich man's new demands is stunningly impressive. When Abraham is describing the fixed chasm, he mentions, 'Those who would pass from here to you may not be able, and none may cross from there to us.'

It is obvious that the rich man would be happy to pass from hell to heaven. But who in heaven would want to descend to hell? The language of the text stimulates us to look for a candidate. The story itself (off stage) suggests one—Lazarus! Lazarus, it seems, is whispering unnoticed in Abraham's ear and is saying, 'Father Abraham, that's my old neighbour down there. If he needs a drink —there is water on the table in front of me—I'll be glad to take it to him!'

Bless those who spitefully use you (cf. Luke 6:27ff). The parable calls on us to focus on the question of *our* responses to the bounty (the rich man) and pain (Lazarus) of life. In those responses we create, for good or evil, meaning for ourselves and for our world.

Psalms

A very large number of the psalms may be classified as 'laments'. In other words they are poems or songs in which the singer expresses to God his sadness, his grief, his anxiety, his puzzlement and even his anger about the circumstances of his life. Sometimes the whole community at worship expresses similar feelings about the events which have befallen the nation. On other occasions it seems that the king speaks on behalf of his people but it is not always easy to tell whether the lament is sung by an ordinary Israelite or by the king in his representative role. There are other psalms in which the king clearly plays a significant part and the demands made upon him are set out.

The psalms we shall read over the next three weeks are chosen with this in mind. In the first week we shall read six personal laments, in the second six national laments and in the third six in which the king plays a significant part.

If this concentration on laments sounds a little depressing, don't be put off. There is more to the psalms than this, for most of them also speak of confidence and hope in God.

The notes are based on the Revised Standard Version but it is always helpful to read another translation alongside, such as the Revised English Bible.

12–18 OCTOBER PERSONAL LAMENTS

1 A psalm for no-hopers *Read Psalm 88*

Of all the laments in the book of Psalms this stands out as the only one which is unrelieved by thoughts of hope or promise. Here, as is usually the case, it is impossible to discern precisely what the psalmist's trouble was. It may have been illness of some kind but, whatever it was, it had been with him for most of his life (v. 15). What we can say is that he feels himself to be on the verge of death. Sheol and the pit are imminent (vv. 3–4). In the Old Testament, these were the place where the dead went, never to return but to exist alone in darkness (Job 10:21–22). So the prospect is grim because not only is there no return, but there he will be out of God's mind and hand (v. 5). Psalm 139 sees God also present even in Sheol, but not this psalmist. What confronts him is emptiness and oblivion (vv. 10–12).

This is not a question of luck or fate; it is God who has brought him to this situation (vv. 6–8). Since he believes in only one God, and he an all-powerful one, there is no one else to blame. It must be an expression of the wrath of God, but he gives no reason for this. He doesn't put it down to punishment for his own sin. It all seems inexplicable. It has deprived him of all his friends, who probably thought it safer not to associate with one so afflicted by God.

So there is only one thing left for him and that is to go on praying to God (vv. 9, 13) and so mantain contact with him. Perhaps this suggests that the psalmist hasn't finally given up all hope, in spite of everything.

Some people do seem to be so badly treated by life for no apparent reason that all they can do is hang on to God by their fingernails.

2 A psalm for the sick *Read Psalm 6*

The immediate cause of this psalmist's distress is certainly illness but, again, any diagnosis is impossible. 'Bones' often stands for the physical body, and so he is on the verge of collapse. The word translated 'soul' does not mean some spiritual part of a person as distinct from the body; it often means 'life' or even 'self'. So the psalmist himself is totally dismayed. In the second half of verse 3, his prayer breaks off and turns into a cry of distress: 'How long will it go on?' Because his illness is not described in detail, the psalm could—and can—be used by others who feel that life is nearly slipping away from them.

As in Psalm 88, the psalmist puts his illness down to God's anger. There is no mention of sin and, later, no hint of repentance. He simply throws himself on the mercy of God and pleads to be delivered from death and Sheol (see Psalm 88:10).

The RSV mentions 'foes' in verse 7 and this is not impossible since illness, because of its connection with the anger of God, often seems to have turned friends into enemies. It may be, however, that the word should be translated 'distress', the depth of which can be measured by his being blinded with tears.

Unlike Psalm 88, however, a remarkable change of tone occurs at verse 8. Such a change is common in these psalms of lament. What is it that convinces him that, in spite of all, God has heard his prayer? It may be that it is just a mood swing; but more likely it is due to some word or action by the priest officiating in worship, an assurance of God's presence and grace.

Whatever else worship is and does, it ought to bring about a meeting between the worshipper and God in which the worshipper is made aware that, whatever the circumstances, God is present to hear our prayers.

3 A psalm when under attack *Read Psalm 64*

This psalmist really is in trouble and it is no wonder that he begins his psalm with a 'complaint' or 'lament'. There is no question about the seriousness of his situation but we are given no clue as to why he was being attacked so ruthlessly. Was it because he had reached a position of which they were envious or from which they felt threatened? We are not told and we can only speculate.

Vicious as the attack may seem, it was verbal and not physical. The language of physical assault is used metaphorically. However, it is no less vicious for that, as his enemies seek to get rid of him one way or another.

The Hebrew text presents some difficulties and verses 5 and 6 should probably be translated:

They encourage themselves with wicked words.
They talk secretly of laying snares,
saying 'Who can see them?'
They have devised all kinds of injustice,
thinking, 'We have made our plans perfectly.'
Their intentions are hidden deep inside them…

Yet the psalmist has an underlying confidence in God's justice, and their secrecy will be of no avail, for nothing can be hidden from God. His retribution in verses 7–8 is precise in its terms. Just as they have aimed words like 'arrows', so God will aim his 'arrow' of judgment against them; just as they shoot 'suddenly', so they will be wounded 'suddenly'; they sharpened their 'tongues' like swords and so he will turn their 'tongues' against them; they may think that no one can 'see' but everyone will 'see'. This 'eye for eye' revenge on God's part may disturb us but, first, it has a useful effect on those who look on and, second, for us it is a reminder that for all our insistence on the love of God we should never forget his justice.

All this allows the psalmist to end very differently from the way he began—on a note of confidence for those who do right.

4 A psalm of mood swings *Read Psalm 22*

It is difficult to separate this psalm from the experience of Jesus on the cross as described by the evangelists. However, it is worth our while to reflect on it for its own sake and on its own terms. It surely represents the ups and downs which most of us feel when confronted by difficulties.

The first two verses describe the psalmist's sense of abandonment by God. It is here that he begins and not with the details of his trouble, for this is where his deepest trouble lies. As against this, he recalls (vv. 3–5) how God has been faithful to his ancestors, helping them in times of trouble. This is insufficient to quell his doubts and he remembers how people make fun of him for continuing to trust even in so much misfortune (vv. 6–8). This drives him back on his own experience of God's help in the past (vv. 9–10) and he prays that it may continue (v. 11).

Still he can't escape from his present trouble. The attacks of his enemies are described in the metaphorical language of wild animals, so that he feels at the point of death (vv. 12–17). How far, if at all, the attacks were physical we cannot say for sure. Certainly they were very fierce but, in spite of his feelings of desertion, the psalmist goes on seeking God's help (vv. 19–21).

At verse 23 the mood changes yet again to one of confident praise. Such a sudden and so great a switch has led some to believe that verses 23–31 were originally a separate psalm. It may be, however, that these verses come from a time when the psalmist's prayers had been answered or, as others think, that in the course of worship he received such a strong awareness of the presence of God that confidence in his presence and power dispelled all his fears and anxieties. Certainly these final verses have worship as their context (v. 26) where his experience can also affect the lives of others.

Did Jesus have the whole psalm in mind when he quoted the opening lines? The mixture of fear and confidence certainly reflects our own experience until confidence finally conquers through our personal encounter with God.

5 Friends, human and divine *Read Psalm 41*

This psalm begins on a note of confidence that God helps the people who take care of the weak. The last line of verse 3 is better translated as 'you turn over his bed for him', that is, to make him more comfortable rather than to heal him. It may sound as though the psalmist is advocating helping the weak in order to secure God's help. Almost certainly he doesn't regard care for the poor as a guarantee of his own health and prosperity. It is simply that it usually works out this way, in many if not in all cases. In any case, in view of the rest of the psalm, it may be that the psalmist is here quoting the generally held view rather than giving his own opinion.

At all events he is prepared to admit that his illness has been brought about by his sin, which he now confesses. What seems to hurt him more, however, is the fact that people gloat over him, whispering to one another that he is about to die, and spreading rumours.

Worse even than that is the fact that his erstwhile friend has behaved in the same way. Was it deliberate rumour-mongering? Or was his friend simply telling others how he saw the situation? To share a meal with another was, and still is, a sign of close friendship and whatever the friend's motives the psalmist sees it as a betrayal of trust.

His final prayer for healing is based on two things: first, his desire to prove his enemies (and his friend?) wrong; and, second, his own integrity—which does not mean that he has not sinned but that he has been honest enough to admit it. The prayer is not just for healing but that he may have a place in God's presence for ever. Nothing could be better than that.

Verse 13 does not belong to this psalm at all. It is a doxology which was used to close the first book of psalms when at some stage the Psalter was divided into five books, perhaps to correspond to the five books of the Law.

6 Faithless friends *Read Psalm 55*

We have already read some psalms in which the psalmist laments the fact that he is under attack from enemies, and in Psalm 41 we saw how he felt betrayed by a friend. Psalm 55 is an even more poignant expression of sadness and anger at the behaviour not just of enemies but of a close friend, and the middle part of the psalm is addressed directly to him (vv. 12–14). They were 'equals', men of the same class and standing. Their friendship was very close. The picture of these two men walking in the temple courts, deep in conversation and thoroughly enjoying each other's company, leaves a strong impression of the closeness of their friendship.

Later in the psalm (vv. 20–21), it appears (in spite of REB) that he speaks again of his friend as one who was at 'peace' with him but who has now, literally, 'broken his covenant'. This suggests a very special bond between them. Did they just happen to be good friends worshipping together? Or were they both perhaps members of the temple staff solemnly bound together by their work and their position? But something had happened. The friend's words still came out as usual but behind them there was treachery and hurt as he sided with the psalmist's enemies.

In spite of the intensity of the bitterness that is evident, two verses in particular have remained in our memory. 'O for the wings of a dove! I would fly away and be at rest' (v. 6)—the overwhelming desire to escape from the machinations of his enemies—and 'Cast your burden on the Lord'—a confession of faith in God's grace and power which forms the basis of his trust. Both often speak to our human need.

GUIDELINES

The psalmists often express thoughts and feelings which are also in our minds and hearts, but which we hide away from other people and try to hide from God because we believe them to be unworthy. Perhaps we need to be reminded again that God reads our thoughts and doesn't depend on what we say. So maybe it is better to be open and honest like the psalmists. At least by complaining to God we are acknowledging that he is there, and by chafing at apparent injustice we are affirming our belief in God's own ultimate justice.

The injustices of life come in different forms—illness, enmity, even treachery of close friends. If we are honest we can share the psalmists' sense of bewilderment and anger. When this happens, sometimes all we can do is 'hang on in there'.

What saves the psalmists from utter despair is the belief that God is there to hear the complaint and the request for justice. In their distress, however great, they are not left alone. Life may be a burden but it may be 'cast on the Lord' and, in the end, he can be trusted. It is when we bottle things up or pretend to ourselves that they are not there that we do damage to ourselves and to other people. To be honest with ourselves and with God about our fears, our doubts, our feelings that we are hard done by, is the first step along the road to peace of mind.

And when the cup you give is filled to brimming
with bitter suffering, hard to understand,
we take it gladly, trusting though with trembling,
out of so good and so beloved a hand.

Dietrich Bonhoeffer

19–25 OCTOBER NATIONAL LAMENTS

1 Whose side is God on? *Read Psalm 44*

This week we are to read psalms which have to do with the fortunes of the nation. The present psalm begins by expressing a view which is common in the Old Testament, namely that victory is not due to military strength but is the gift of God. At the Reed Sea (a more accurate translation than Red Sea) the Israelites had only to stand still—'The Lord will fight for you' (Exodus 14:14); at the fall of Jericho when the walls fell at the sound of the trumpets, 'I have given Jericho into your hands' (Joshua 6:2); in the days of the Judges, Gideon, who belonged to the weakest clan, had to send his most efficient soldiers home, so that it would be clear that God had given victory (Judges 7:2–8). It is always God who gives victory to his people.

There is nothing in this psalm to say what the actual situation was in which it was first used, but it was doubtless used on other similar occasions too. The fact that the psalm sometimes slips into the singular suggests that it was sung by an individual on behalf of the people, and some people think that individual was the king.

The 'Yet…' in verse 9 brings us to the heart of the psalm. It is all very well to trust in God to give victory but what happens when the nation is defeated? Of course, their conquerors make fun of them and taunt them. It would be easy to put it down to unfaithfulness on the part of the nation, but the psalmist is not aware of any serious breach of the commandment to worship God alone (vv. 17–18). Can it be that God has fallen asleep and so is unaware of their situation? Has he turned his back on them? (vv. 23–24)

There is no answer to these questions. All the people can do is to call on God to help as a sign of his devotion. God's failure to act in the way we expect remains a mystery for both individuals and for whole peoples.

2 The holy city defiled *Read Psalm 74*

The psalm begins with that worrying question, 'Why?' It's the question we are all tempted to ask when things do not go as we expect. Again the situation is one of defeat but this time we may be fairly sure that the psalm was composed after Nebuchadnezzar's capture of Jerusalem and destruction of the temple in 587BC. It was probably used again in the second century BC when Antiochus IV Epiphanes again sacked the city and temple. The psalm has to be understood against the background of the promise to David in 2 Samuel 7 and the consequent belief that Jerusalem, as the dwelling-place of God, could never be captured or destroyed (cf. Psalm 46).

The call to God to remember (v. 2) is more than a jogging of his memory; it is an invitation to act on the basis of what was remembered.

The description of the devastation poses some difficulties for translators but the general picture is clear. The enemy has set up his standards as a sign of victory and then laid waste the temple. Jeremiah the prophet had foreseen this but was now no longer around, having been carried off to Egypt. He had said the exile in Babylon would last for some time but, 'How long?' they ask and, again, 'Why?' (vv 10–11)

Remarkably, these momentous events do not destroy the psalmist's faith in God as king, which he now confesses again (v. 12). Using the language of old creation myths (the dragons and Leviathan), he affirms his belief in God as creator (vv. 13–14) and sustainer (vv. 15–17). On the basis of this belief he seeks retribution upon the enemy. 'Dove' (v. 19) had already been used as a simile for Israel (Hosea 7:11) and is perhaps taken up again in the book of Jonah, whose name, in Hebrew, means 'dove'. If the word 'covenant' is correct in verse 20 it would refer to the promise to David in 2 Samuel 7, though it is probably better to translate the phrase as 'those who feed on oppression'.

It is perhaps curious that no mention is made of the deportation of people to Babylon. Could it be that some verses which did so in the original version were omitted when the psalm was re-used in the Maccabean period?

The request for God to intervene is not merely a matter of revenge or even restoration. More importantly, what is at stake for the psalmist is God's name, that is, his holy reputation.

3 Quiet confidence *Read Psalms 123 and 124*

These two psalms belong to a group of psalms, each headed 'A Song of Ascents'. This probably means that they came to be used by Israelites when on pilgrimage to Jerusalem. Both psalms are full of quiet confidence, although 123 presupposes a time of hardship and 124 gives thanks for deliverance. There is nothing in either psalm to indicate what the difficult situation was. We should not be surprised at this because if they were too specific they would not be suitable for use on other occasions. In 123 there is a plea for help but it hasn't the agonized ugency that we have met in other psalms. The similes used in verse 2 show just how confidently the psalmist could appeal to God for help, whatever the nation's need might be. He begins not by dwelling on the difficulties but by reminding the worshippers of the God whom they worship. He is the king of all creation and so can be trusted.

In Psalm 124 the leader of the congregation recites the first line of the psalm and then invites the congregation to join in, which they do in verse 2. The theme of the psalm is clear enough. We saw in Psalm 44 the belief that victory depended entirely on the presence and support of the Lord. Here too, without the help of God they would have been overrun by enemies.

'Blessed be the Lord' has become almost a religious cliché. The word 'blessing' when applied to God in this way has more to do with thanks than with any gift we can give to him. We could translate this as 'Thanks be to the Lord.'

The closing verse of the psalm is very similar to Psalm 121:2. Confidence in God is founded on his power as creator and on his faithfulness in times of trouble.

4 The meeting of heaven and earth *Read Psalm 85*

If we want to find the context in which this psalm was sung, we have to look to verses 4–6 with their plea to 'restore us'. There is no mention of enemies here. It is possible that 'revive us' in verse 6 suggests a time of famine or drought, but the psalm is vague enough to be used in any number of situations. What is noticeable is that the psalmist attributes the problem to the anger of God and, in the light of verse 2, we must assume that this was on account of his people's sin.

Once again, the psalmist doesn't launch immediately into a description of the people's problem. He begins, where all worship should, with God. Looking to the past, he is able to recall how God had 'restored the fortunes' of his people. The phrase came to be used especially for the return from exile in Babylon and we are reminded by the book of Haggai that this was followed by a time of famine brought about by neglect of God through their own selfish concerns. These are things which are likely to happen again and again, and so the psalm is appropriate now as then.

Verses 8–9 are spoken by a leader of the congregation, perhaps by a temple prophet. As prophets did, he listened for the word of God and expects a word of 'peace', *shalom*, well-being to those who turn to him and show him reverence. The glory which is promised is nothing other than the presence of God himself. The word is often, though not always, associated with the ark of the covenant, the throne of God.

In verses 10–11 various qualities are personified in a poetic fashion. Devotion (RSV, 'steadfast love') and righteousness (right behaviour) coming from God will be met by faithfulness and peace coming from his people. Then ideal conditions will ensue. The last line should probably read '…and peace will follow in his footsteps'.

Human confession and divine forgiveness, followed by a proper response to the grace of God, may not always relieve famine but will produce an experience of *shalom*, peace.

5 A Passover psalm *Read Psalm 115*

There is no direct reference to the deliverance from Egypt, which was traditionally remembered at Passover. Indeed there are certain features of this psalm which suggest that it was composed to celebrate some later deliverance, such as the return from exile in Babylon. Nevertheless, it could be used appropriately as one of a group of psalms sung at Passover.

The psalm makes good sense once we realize that it is a piece of liturgy in which different people take part. Verses 1–3, sung by the whole congregation, turn attention away from the worshippers themselves towards God, whose salvation and power they celebrate. This is where all worship should begin.

Verses 4–8 remind us of passages from the great prophet of the exile such as Isaiah 40:18–20, 44:9–20 and 46:1–7. They may well have been sung by a temple prophet or some other representative figure. They conclude with the percipient observation that worshippers tend to become like the object of their worship.

In verses 9–11 the prophet calls on people, priests and 'fearers of the Lord' to trust him, and there is a response to each call. The 'fearers' may be converts to Judaism.

On the basis of such trust, a priest is able to offer a priestly blessing (vv. 12–15). Blessing from God usually implies some quite concrete benefit and not just a vague wish. Verse 14 mentions particularly fertility and we should remember that the highest blessing for a woman was to have seven sons!

Finally, in verses 16–18, the whole congregation joins in a hymn of praise. There is a reminder of the emptiness and silence of Sheol and so it is right to praise God while the opportunity remains. In the light of the resurrection we do not share this rather pessimistic view but the encouragement to thank and praise God is still needed so that we may join in his final 'Hallelujah'—praise the Lord.

6 A king speaks for his people *Read Psalm 60*

Clearly this psalm reflects a time of national emergency but, as with other psalms we have studied, the precise circumstances cannot be known. As we have seen, liturgical material needs to be general rather than particluar so that it may be used again and again in different situations. The heading to the psalm in RSV is a later attempt to fit it into the life of David and it has no real historical value.

It seems that the land is under attack and this is put down to God's anger with his people and his rejection of them. The plea is therefore for restoration. The Hebrew of verse 4 is somewhat obscure. Rather than God setting up a rallying point for his people (RSV), it more likely continues the theme of danger. It may be translated:

> ***You have given a signal to your warriors***
> ***to take flight before the enemy archers.***

Then verse 5 is a cry for deliverance: 'May thy beloved...'

The remainder of the psalm (vv. 6–12) is found again as part of Psalm 108, where it has been joined to Psalm 57:8–12 to make a new psalm. At first sight it does not seem to sit comfortably with what has gone before in this present psalm. However, it does make sense if we see verses 6–8 as words spoken by a prophet in the temple, recalling the old traditions about the possession and distribution of the promised land among the tribes, and the authority they will have over neighbouring nations such as Moab, Edom and Philistia. So understood, these verses are meant to restore confidence in God.

The concluding verses (9–12) mention Edom again, either

literally (the Edomites occupied much of Judah during the exile in Babylon) or metaphorically. Verses 10–12 reiterate what we have seen many times in these psalms, namely that human resources are never sufficient. Without God's help and presence, the situation is hopeless but, conversely and positively, with God's help victory is assured.

Did you notice that in verse 9 we find the singular 'me'? This probably indicated that the first five and last three verses were sung by the king as representing his people.

GUIDELINES

The psalms we have read this week have all been concerned with national events and affairs and they are based on the belief that there was a special relationship between God and Israel. We cannot therefore apply them directly to our own or any other nation. They do, however, refer to corporate life and belief and so we must ask what is the modern, corporate equivalent of Israel. The New Testament sometimes suggests that the Church is the new Israel, called by God and responsible to him like the old Israel (1 Peter 2:9). For the Church, however, psalms of military conquest or defence have no literal relevance, although we do still use military language metaphorically. All this means we must use these psalms with care. Then they have much to say to the Church both local and universal.

First, they remind us of its vulnerability, its fallibility and its weakness. Alongside that, they remind us also of the nature of God as creator and king. Put these two things together and we are shown again our dependence upon God and are urged to trust him for guidance and help. Management techniques alone will not suffice. God alone can bring in his kingdom using the gifts he has given us, when they are placed at his disposal.

Second, they speak to us of the need for corporate worship which should be a constant reminder of these things. The focal point of worship, as they reflect it, is not the congregation but God, and it is upon him that we must rely and it is him whom we should praise. Yet in worship there ought to be honesty, and honest expression of feeling. Sometimes there will be feelings of doubt or even anger or despair but by putting God at the centre of our worship these begin to be dispersed. Such psalms as these help us to express our feelings and come to terms with them.

True, 'tis a strait and thorny road
and mortal spirits tire and faint,
but they forget the mighty God
who feeds the strength of every saint…

From thee, the ever-flowing spring,
our souls shall drink a fresh supply,
while such as trust their native strength
shall faint away and droop and die.

Isaac Watts

26 OCTOBER–1 NOVEMBER ROYAL PSALMS

1 For the coronation of a king *Read Psalm 2*

We have already indicated that some of the 'national' psalms may have been sung by the king as representative of his people. This week we read a group of psalms clearly about the king.

The present psalm is almost certainly one which was used at the accession or coronation of kings in Judah. When a king died, there was often a period of unrest. Other nations took advantage of the situation, especially to break free of any obligations they may have had. It is this that is described in verses 1–3, where it is seen not only as opposition to the king, the anointed, but to the Lord who made him king, a fact which is reaffirmed in verse 6.

Then, in verses 7–9 the king himself recites the divine 'decree' which assures him of the throne. The coronation, what happened 'today', brought the king into a special, close relationship with God which was best expressed in terms of father and son. Because God's rule is universal, so ideally must be that of his 'son', the king, but it remained an ideal, not a reality.

The closing verses (10–12) were spoken by a prophet in the temple, calling upon the other nations to submit to the newly crowned king. The Hebrew translated 'with trembling kiss his feet' in RSV is very difficult and many other translations have been suggested. Almost certainly the other nations are meant to pay homage to the king.

After the exile in Babylon, Judah had no king. This psalm, along with others, was preserved, and not just as a piece of old poetry. It was reinterpreted as referring to the 'anointed one', the Messiah hoped for and expected in the future. Verses from it were then used in the New Testament in reference to Jesus at his baptism (Matthew 3:17), the transfiguration (Matthew 17:5) and the resurrection (Acts 13:33) where the Father–Son relationship between God and Jesus is emphasized.

2 A prayer for royal justice *Read Psalm 72*

This is a long prayer for the king, but although from time to time the prayer is for his personal power (vv. 8–11) or wealth (vv. 15–17) it is much more a prayer that he may reign in such a way as to bring well-being upon the whole nation. It is a prayer for good government, the consequence of which will be prosperity for all.

It is recognized that such an ability to govern well is a gift from God. The justice and righteousness which are required come from him. In Isaiah 11:1ff the same qualities are attributed to the Spirit, the power of God. 'Righteousness' in the Old Testament generally means fulfilling one's obligations to others and 'justice' is the overall context in which this happens. Such obligations are based on the fact that the people, including the king, are the people of God and therefore related to each other through their common dependence on and allegiance to God. What we find, therefore, both in this psalm and in the prophetic books, is not a call to the poor to stand up for their rights, but a demand upon the rich and powerful to fulfil their obligations.

The king was responsible for seeing to it that this kind of righteousness and justice was a feature of the nation over whom he ruled. In this psalm, therefore, the people pray that the king may be enabled to rule in this way so that peace and prosperity for people and king alike may flourish.

The prayers for the king's personal well-being in verses 5–11 and 15–17 are expressed in wonderfully poetic terms—long life, worldwide authority, wealth and a lasting reputation. However, such prayers for 'blessing' are mixed with those for justice. The two things are inseparable in the thought of the psalmist.

Again we must assume that, when there was no longer a king in Judah, this psalm also looked forward to the coming one, the Messiah.

Verses 18–20 do not form a part of this psalm. Like those at the end of Psalm 41 they are a doxology composed later to close a book of the Psalter at a time when it was divided into five books, perhaps to correspond with the five books of the Law.

3 In praise of the king *Read Psalm 21*

Clearly this psalm was sung in times of prosperity and peace. Indeed it probably celebrated victory, for the word rendered 'help' in RSV really means 'deliverance' or 'victory' (see REB). We have no means of knowing what the original occasion was but in any case the psalm would have been used on other similar occasions.

The first six verses are addressed to the king but consistently the king's success is attributed to God, and any fame he may acquire is not a result of his own effort but a gift from God.

Since verse 7 speaks of both the king and God in the third person, it may well have been used as a response by the congregation.

Verses 8–12 are again addressed to the king, giving him assurance of future victory over enemies but, once more, verse 9 makes it clear that this will be the Lord's doing. Therefore, the psalm ends on a note of praise to God and not to the king. The threats against the children of enemies (v. 10) strike us as cruelly vindictive and we find it hard to repeat such words. We have to remember that the only way a person could be thought to live on after death was through his reputation (name) or offspring. So the annihilation of the Lord's enemies could be accomplished only when their children were also destroyed. This does not make it any easier for us to use such threats but at least it helps us to understand why they were made. For us they need serious revision in the light of the Christian gospel.

The reference to the crown and the gift of life in verses 3 and 4 has led some to think not so much of a military victory but of a temple ritual, held annually, in which the king, representing his people, was humiliated and ritually 'died' before being brought to life again by God and re-crowned king. There is some evidence that such a ritual may have taken place in Jerusalem. This does not alter the fact that the king owes his position to God and it is therefore God who is to be praised.

4 The king at worship *Read Psalm 132*

This psalm also makes excellent sense once it is seen as a piece of temple liturgy. It falls neatly into two halves, each ending with a kind of refrain in verses 9 and 16. The first part recalls David's promise to God and the second God's promise to David.

The first part is based upon the events in 2 Samuel 6 where David brought the ark into Jerusalem, though there is no actual mention of a promise in that chapter. Ephrathah is associated with Bethlehem, David's birthplace, in Micah 5:2, while Jaar is to be identified with Kiriath-jearim where David found the ark. Passages such as this and the one in Psalm 68:25–29 suggest that the bringing of the ark into Jerusalem was re-enacted annually, the ark being taken in procession round the city and then brought back into it.

The second part (vv. 11–16) is based on 2 Samuel 7, where God promised to David that a descendant of his would sit on the throne for ever. This was coupled with a demand for obedience. With the ark, God's throne, and the king, God's anointed, safely in Jerusalem again, the city could expect prosperity.

The refrain in verses 9 and 16 pictures the priests dressed in righteousness—that is, doing what is right—and the devoted servants (RSV, 'saints') singing for joy.

The final verses (17–18) seem to suggest there is no longer a king to be acclaimed. Instead they look forward to one whom God will raise up. It seems very likely that these verses were added to make the psalm still usable when the people were in exile in Babylon. They could no longer process with the ark into Jerusalem or acclaim the king, so they reinterpreted it to look forward, once again, to the future with hopes of a return to Zion and the restoration of the monarchy. That future was never fully realized but an 'anointed one' was still expected. Christians found this messianic hope fulfilled in Jesus.

The psalm then reminds us of our promise to give God pride of place in our lives and of God's promise fulfilled in Jesus our king.

5 The divine king's city *Read Psalm 48*

This psalm is different from those we have read so far this week. Here it is God who is king. There was in Israel something of a conflict between a human king and the Lord, the divine king. This is reflected in a passage like 1 Samuel 8:4–9. It was resolved to some extent by regarding the king as a kind of 'adopted' son of God, owing his kingship to God, responsible to him and dependent on him. We saw this in Psalm 2.

This psalm therefore celebrated the fact that the Lord is king and Zion is not simply the national capital but the home of the Lord. So the first three verses sing the praises of the city. It is unlikely that Jerusalem could be described as being 'in the far north'. The Hebrew word for 'north' is *Zaphon* and this was the name of the mountain where the Canaanite gods were supposed to live. Here it is used metaphorically of the home of Israel's God.

The following verses, 4–11, seem to presuppose some special activity in the temple which was seen by Judeans and foreigners alike and which produced a sense of awe. Since the psalm is closely related to Psalms 46 and 47, we may surmise that there was some ceremony in which the kingship of the Lord was reaffirmed. Psalms 93 and 95–99 may belong to the same ceremony. The verb translated 'we have thought on' (RSV) or 'we meditate on' (REB) may be translated 'we have portrayed' and this would support some such re-enactment.

The final verses seem to refer to and reflect on a procession around Jerusalem such as we met in Psalm 132. The 'this' in verse 14 is quite emphatic and may be thought to point to the ark where God, the invisible king, was enthroned.

In the end, therefore, it is not Jerusalem which is to be praised for its own sake. What makes it a city to be praised is the fact that in it God is acknowledged as king. We may ask ourselves whether this has something to say about the Church.

6 The divine king's demands *Read Psalm 95*

Finally we come to a psalm the first part of which is very well-known and widely used as a call to worship. It has often been paraphrased in our hymns. In fact there are two calls to worship. The first, in verses 1–5, calls people to worship God as creator, a fact which shows his kingship and his supremacy. It is sometimes thought that this is a call to enter the outer court of the temple. The second, in verses 6–7, is then seen as a further invitation into the inner court. This would be addressed specifically to Israelites, for in these verses God is praised not as the creator of the world but as the creator of Israel. They had become God's people when he brought them out of Egypt. So now their response is not just a song of praise but an act of humble obeisance before their maker. The figure of sheep and shepherd is common enough in the Old Testament referring to a king and his people, but here specifically to God and his people as in Ezekiel 34.

These invitations are followed by verses which we rarely hear read in church. Nevertheless, they are an integral part of the psalm. This warning was probably given by a temple official, perhaps a prophet or a Levite. It is intended for the present worshippers ('today'). They are to avoid the mistakes of their ancestors. To 'harden the heart' is to become stubborn, self-willed and disobedient. The traditions about Meribah and Massah are rather complicated, but here the passages in mind would be Exodus 17:1–7 and Deuteronomy 33:8. The two places received their names because at Massah, which means 'questioning', they questioned God's ability to provide water in the desert. So they went their own way instead of trusting God (Meribah means 'rebellion'). Consequently they failed to enter the 'rest', the promised land. Likewise, present worshippers will fail to reach their 'rest' if they question God's will and follow their own.

Worship involves more than singing hymns of praise, more even than the humble recognition of God who made us his own. It involves trust and obedience in all areas of life.

GUIDELINES

It may be tempting to apply the message of these royal psalms to the monarchy today. This will not do because the role of the king was very different in those days. It is possible, however, to see in them some guidance concerning government in the wider sense. These psalms make it clear that the responsibility of those who govern is to do so in 'righteousness'. This means fulfilling those obligations towards our neighbours which we incur as members of the community in which we live, expecially towards the less fortunate.

We should remember, however, that the society in question in the psalms is the people of God, and we who are the people of God today are bound to think of the Church. Sometimes, as in 1 Peter 2:9–10, the Church seems to be regarded as a new Israel. In this case the psalms have something to say about leadership in the Church, an issue which keeps on coming to the fore. Within the Church, leadership implies service and the pursuit of 'righteousness'. Moreover, the psalms remind us that leaders are appointed by God and are both responsible to and dependent on him. This leaves no room for pride or self-aggrandizement.

We have seen that the psalms continued to be used even when there was no king in Israel. Then they were sung as referring to a future king. It is therefore legitimate for Christians to think of Jesus as the fulfilment of that hope, as the expected king whose rule must be acknowledged both individually and corporately.

The coming of Jesus brought the kingdom of God to the present world and yet its fulfilment is still future—'Thy kingdom come'. Then people will obey his rule—'Thy will be done'. The last two psalms point beyond the human king to the fact that God, the creator of the world and of the chosen people, is to be worshipped and obeyed. This causes no conflict for the Christian for we believe that Jesus is the divine Son of God, and so there is no distinction between the kingship of Jesus and that of God the Father.

We may still look forward with the psalmists to a future time when God's rule, exercised through his Son, will be acknowledged by all people who will live together in 'righteousness', each doing what he ought to do for the other. Then will follow that 'rest', the time of *shalom*, of peace and well-being.

> *For us the meaning of the kingdom of God is seen far and away more clearly in the person of Jesus himself than in any definition he gave of it. He gave its secret away by the sort of things he did and the sort of words he spoke, by the way he prayed and the way he preached and the way he healed, above all by the way he suffered and the way he died and the way he rose again.*
>
> *J.E. Fison*

The Gospel of John Chapters 7–12

Our readings so far in this gospel have taken us halfway through its first part, often called 'The Book of Signs'. Jesus has journeyed from Judea to Galilee, then from Galilee to Jerusalem and back, via Samaria. His teaching has been received, but also rejected. His signs have evoked faith, but also opposition. He has insisted that life lies at the heart of Moses' teaching, but Moses' interpreters have begun to look for ways of killing him.

This next section of the gospel, the second half of the Book of Signs, has Jesus mostly in Jerusalem. It is the scene of fierce debate with the Jewish authorities, and Jesus has to flee for his life on more than one occasion. But as the narrative progresses, he emerges not as the victim of his enemies' intention to take his life from him, but as one who is supremely free to give his life for the salvation of the world.

The notes are based on the Revised Standard Version of the Bible.

2–8 NOVEMBER JOHN 7:1—8:20

1 To Jerusalem? *Read John 7:1–13*

On the face of it, 'after this' refers back to the previous chapter and the discourse in the synagogue at Capernaum. But the note of hostility towards Jesus fits in better with chapter 5, when he was last in Jerusalem and the Jewish leaders tried to kill him (see 5:16–18). Understandably Jesus is now wary of travelling to Jerusalem publicly as a pilgrim to the Feast of Tabernacles (or 'booths'). This was the most popular Jewish festival. It lasted for a week in late September–early October, and commemorated Israel's living in tents during their time in the wilderness (see Leviticus 23:33ff).

The statement that 'my time has not yet come' and the reference to the world that 'hates me because I testify of it that its works are evil' elevates Jesus' hesitancy above the proper concern to avoid danger. What has already taken place in Jerusalem anticipates his destiny, for which an imminent visit to the city is 'not yet' the moment. Jesus may be unwilling to take his brothers' advice for other reasons. He has already shown himself reluctant to trust himself to those, in Jerusalem and elsewhere, whose faith relies too much on his works of healing and feeding (2:23ff; 6:26). The kind of faith he looks for is found in the characters we met in chapter 4—the Samaritan woman and the official in Capernaum. True faith recognizes Jesus as messiah and relies on his word, with its power to bring life in the face of death. If this faith is lacking in his brothers, why should he take their advice?

But then he does go to Jerusalem privately, apart from the pilgrims. There is an elusiveness about Jesus here, as we saw after the feeding in Galilee (6:15, 24). This is matched by the clandestine way in which opinions about him circulate in the city. As in Capernaum, his teaching has opened up a division in his audience. Is he 'good' (that is, acting with God's authority; compare Mark 10:17–18: 'Good teacher ... no one is good but God alone'), or a false prophet who leads the people astray by undermining the demand for sabbath obedience?

There is more to Jesus' elusiveness than avoiding danger. His approach says something about the kind of revelation he brings, and the way to apprehend it. Miracles of healing and feeding are as ambiguous as they are impressive. They may be perceived as divine or diabolical, acts of mercy or works of magic. They are not sufficient to establish Jesus' credentials. Even his teachings may be received as no more than the rantings of one deluded by his own sense of divinity. Divided opinion is inevitable in the face of the indirect way God chooses to reveal himself in the Word made flesh. Faith—the response Jesus looks for—trusts in the integrity of his words and deeds. This is risky, because there is no assured outcome at the beginning of the journey of faith. Assurance only grows along the way.

2 In the temple *Read John 7:14–24*

Surprisingly, in view of the danger and his desire to avoid pre-empting his destiny, Jesus now appears in public. But he does not entirely shed his elusiveness, as the public's question shifts from 'where is he?' to 'where does he get his teaching from?' Jesus does not identify with one of the well-known scribal schools. If he did, the public would be able to judge his message by relating it to this or that version of recognized Jewish teaching. As it is, he insists on appealing directly to God: his teaching comes from 'him who sent me'. We can imagine how his words in verses 17 and 18 can only infuriate the Jewish leaders. They too see themselves as pursuing the will of God and seeking his glory.

How can Jesus and his opponents resolve their differences when each claims to be consistent with scripture and faithful to the law of Moses? Jesus has earlier charged the Jewish leaders with failing to believe Moses' writings (5:46). Now he accuses the people of defaulting on the law because they want to kill him. At first sight his assertion that 'none of you keeps the law' looks like an over-generalization. Perhaps he means that his opponents have missed what he perceives as the true spirit of the law. They focus on those parts of the law—circumcision and sabbath—which had become particularly important for Jews who understood holiness in terms of separation from a world that they believed was unclean. This sectarian response is entirely understandable in the face of the spread of Greek culture and Roman rule to Palestine. But for Jesus it is inadequate. It is a recipe for inconsistency. It insists that the sabbath should be kept free of work, yet allows an eight-day-old boy to be circumcised on the sabbath, while forbidding the healing of a man paralysed for thirty-eight years (verse 23 refers back to 5:1–18). And it narrows down God's concern to maintaining sectarian holiness rather than conferring life itself. Notice the irony: those who miss the true spirit of the law find themselves resorting to violence.

'Do not judge by appearances, but judge with right judgment' (v. 24). For Jesus, it is immaterial whether a teacher is backed by the honour of a particular scribal school or a powerful personal authority. These things are no more than appearances which at best enhance an individual's status. What really matters is not a teacher's claim to be doing the will of God, but his understanding of the scope of God's will. According to Jesus, God's interest is much wider than the separatist holiness symbolized by the temple in which he delivers his teaching. Israel's God is the God of life—

the whole person, the whole community, the whole world. Reading the law with this in mind will deliver right judgment.

3 Where is he from? Where is he going? *Read John 7:25–36*

Now it is the mind of the Jewish authorities that proves to be elusive: what are the pilgrims in Jerusalem to make of their allowing Jesus to speak so openly? Whatever the authorities really think, the public are in no doubt. Some 'judge by appearances' (v. 24), and know enough about Jesus' background and origins to convince them that he cannot possibly be the messiah. They remind us of characters we have already met in the gospel—the Jews in Capernaum who judge Jesus by his parentage (6:42). Others 'judge with right judgment' and see the true significance of his signs. The abundance of wine (2:1–11), the overcoming of death (4:46–54) and the healing of paralysis (5:1–18) belong with the messianic age of salvation, when God renews the life of Israel and through them the world (Isaiah 25:6–8; 35:5–7).

Jesus' now familiar claim to be speaking and acting for God is lifted on to a higher plane with his talk of 'going to him who sent me' (v. 33). The Jewish leaders are puzzled, and think only in terms of his leaving Palestine to visit Jewish communities elsewhere—in Alexandria perhaps, or Babylon, or one of the cities around the Mediterranean. The alert reader will spot the descent–ascent motif in Jesus' talk of coming from and returning to God. The motif is accompanied by official action against Jesus, as the Pharisees and chief priests try to have him arrested. There is a clear reminder here that Jesus' passion is the result not only of opposition to his teaching but also deep-seated ignorance of the source of his authority. In their pursuit of sectarian holiness, the Jewish authorities have lost sight of God. 'Where I am you cannot come' echoes Jesus' earlier condemnation of the leaders of his own people: 'His voice you have never heard, his form you have never seen; you do not have his word abiding in you ... you do not have the love of God within you' (5:37–42).

For all their learning and honour, the leaders of Israel have turned a mechanism for survival in a threatening world (sectarian holiness) into a vision of an inflexible divine will. Now it appears that some of the pilgrims are more in tune with God than their teachers.

4 From Galilee, not Bethlehem *Read John 7:37–52*

Jesus' promise of living water should be set in the context of the festival's ritual, in which water played a prominent part. Prayers were offered for rain, and water was carried in procession from the pool of Siloam into the temple. As the priest poured it over the altar of sacrifice, temple singers chanted words from Isaiah 12:3: 'With joy you shall draw water from the well of salvation'. At the climax of the feast Jesus declares that he is not only the symbol of salvation but also its substance: 'If anyone thirst, let him come *to me* and drink'. We have heard words like these before, in Jesus' conversation with the woman in Sychar (4:14).

Out of *whose* heart do the rivers of living water flow? In verse 37 Jesus refers to himself as the source of living water. Verse 39 underlines this by pointing forward to Jesus' passion, when water flows from his side (19:34), and the risen Christ breathes the Spirit on to his disciples (20:22). But 'out of his heart' parallels 'he who believes in me', and in 4:14 the spring of living water wells up in the thirsty one who drinks the water Jesus gives. 'The scripture' does not settle the issue: the precise reference is hard to identify, and the main contenders (e.g. Isaiah 44:3, 55:1, 58:11) allow the question to be answered either way. Perhaps the ambiguity is deliberate: water/Spirit flows from Jesus into believers and through them. Jesus' gift does not merely satisfy spiritual thirst: it is the source of mission.

Jesus' words again provoke division. There is evidence that rabbis expected the messiah to bring abundant water to Jerusalem, on the basis of Joel 3:18: 'In that day ... all the stream beds of Judah shall flow with water; and a fountain shall come forth from the house of the Lord and water the valley of Shittim'. But some see Jesus' lack of connection with the house of David as decisive. It is interesting that, unlike the birth stories in Matthew and Luke, this gospel makes no attempt to counter these reservations.

The positive impression made on the temple police only serves to draw out the arrogance of the authorities and their contempt for the crowds. The leaders identify truth and right judgment with their own opinion. They refuse to allow that outsiders—those like the pilgrims and Jesus who come from Galilee—might have anything to contribute to the search for truth. The crowds may not know the law in the way that the authorities know it—after all, their knowledge depends on privileged access to the fruits of study—but perhaps the crowds know it in another way. They discern that the essential spirit of the law is life, hence their attraction to Jesus, who utters the word of life, and is the bread of life, and brings the water of life.

Not all members of the Jewish ruling council are so arrogant and contemptuous. But Nicodemus' sympathetic plea that Jesus should at least be given a fair hearing falls on deaf ears. So strong is the authorities' judgment of Jesus according to his earthly origins and background that there is no possibility of their seeing him as the Word made flesh. 'He came to his own home, and his own people received him not' (1:11).

5 In adultery *Read John 7:53—8:11*

The footnote in your Bible reveals that this passage is a free-floating story in the gospel tradition. The incident obstructs the flow of the narrative. And a number of its features have more in common with the synoptic gospels: for example, the reference to 'the scribes and Pharisees', their bringing a disputed legal issue to Jesus 'to test him', and Jesus' refusal to be drawn. Nevertheless, there are some points of contact with this part of John's Gospel. The incident is set in Jerusalem. It shows rising hostility between Jesus and the authorities. And the issues behind the test question—the relationship between the law and life; the matter of whether Jesus sets himself above the law, and so opens himself up to the charge of leading the people astray—have been rehearsed in the previous chapters. Though unlikely to be an original part of John's Gospel, this is as good a home as any for these verses.

There are two other puzzling features of the story. Why does Jesus write on the ground before and after his answer? Some reckon he is embarrassed by the woman, which is improbable in view of his friendship with tax-collectors and notorious sinners. Others think he is writing out verses from the law, or following the Roman custom of setting out his sentence before delivering it. Is he perhaps doodling in the dust, taking time to measure his response? Or maybe he is being typically elusive, refusing to pronounce judgment, in keeping with his words in 8:15: 'I judge no one.'

What is Jesus getting at when he says, 'Let him who is without sin among you be the first to throw a stone at her'? By deserting Jesus and the woman, her accusers as good as admit their guilt. But what sin have they committed? If not adultery, then certainly misreading the law. According to Leviticus 20:10 and Deuteronomy 22:22–24, both parties are guilty of sin in a case like this, and both are to be stoned. If the woman was caught in the act of adultery, what has happened to her partner? She is a victim of male prejudice, a sin which Jesus detects in those who place her in the midst, and one which he condemns in his teaching on divorce in Mark 10:1ff. And in the wider context of the gospel narrative, by wanting to have her stoned her accusers sin against the law of life.

Jesus met another woman with a rather chaotic sexual history, at Sychar (4:17f). He condemns neither. But he does not condone adultery. His generosity towards the Samaritan woman led to spiritual growth. We know nothing of the impact of his compassion on the woman here—not surprisingly, if this is not a genuine Johannine story. We are simply left to wonder whether or not his attitude provided sufficient motivation for moral reform and the development of faith.

6 Light into darkness *Read John 8:12–20*

Jesus' identification with light is well-established in John's Gospel (see 1:4–9; 3:19–21). His saying picks up one of the rituals of Tabernacles. On the first day of the feast, there was a ceremony of lights in which four large candles were lit in the temple's Court of Women. These reputedly illuminated the whole of Jerusalem. But the light of Jesus extends to 'the world'.

Light is a powerful religious metaphor. God is widely associated with light. For the rabbis, so is the Law (after Psalm 119:105: 'Thy word is a lamp to my feet and a light to my path'). Some Jews used Light as a name for the messiah. Zechariah 14:7–8 expects 'the day of the Lord' to bring 'continuous day' to Jerusalem—'for at evening time there shall be light'—as well as living waters flowing out of the holy city. 'Light of the world … light of life' summarizes a key theme in the Gospel. Jesus is the revealer of God, the bringer of salvation, the world's guide.

The Pharisees put Jesus on trial once again. They take exception both to *the fact* and *the error* of his testimony to himself. Notice how Jesus defends himself here, compared to his earlier words in 5:31ff. There he drew on four witnesses to support his claim to be doing God's work. Here he claims the right to bear witness to himself and sit in judgment on his accusers, based on his superior spiritual insight. 'I know ... *but you do not know* whence I have come and whither I am going'. Not that he exercises these rights. He continues to maintain that the Father supports his testimony. And he insists: 'I judge no one.'

Jesus' words are puzzling at first sight. In a sense he *does* exercise judgment. The fact that 'light has come into the world and men loved darkness rather than light' is 'the judgment'. His mission divides humankind into those who do 'what is true' and 'everyone who does evil' (3:19–21). According to 5:22, 'the Father ... has given all judgment to the Son'. The presence of Jesus—the 'light' of his words and works—exposes the particular forms of evil we have met in the Gospel narrative, notably the way the Jewish leaders use their power, and narrow down the significance of the law to justify their sectarian view of the world. It is certainly true that Jesus does not judge as his opponents judge—'according to the flesh', that is, by the estimates of human honour and worth. Because his judgment is not obscured by such preoccupations, his knowledge of the true source and goal of his life and work can be trusted. It shines like light into darkness: revealing, exposing, saving, guiding.

GUIDELINES

Leaders are always tempted to believe that they know best. This is true of religious leaders, politicians, parents, community activists and international financiers. Sometimes exercises in consultation only succeed in masking this form of arrogance.

Jesus didn't shirk at insisting on his own authority. He didn't embark on a consultation process to find out what would be acceptable to the masses. But he wasn't guilty of arrogance. He was blessed by an integrity of word and deed which supported his claim to be acting with the authority of the God of life. He provides a standard against which all leadership is judged.

Lord, save our leaders from the delusion
that their position automatically confers knowledge
and wisdom.
Bless them with the humility and integrity
which earn respect for their insight.

9–15 NOVEMBER JOHN 8:21—9:34

1 From above, from below *Read John 8:21–30*

The conflict between Jesus and the Jewish authorities continues to intensify. There have been strong hints that this will bring about Jesus' passion. But for the moment, the evangelist is content to keep us in suspense (v. 20). In yesterday's passage Jesus started to turn the spotlight on his accusers. Now this also intensifies with his statement in verse 21: his words generate a series of questions which lay bare all that divides him from his accusers.

'Where I am going, you cannot come.' The Jews have already asked whether he intends to take his mission to Greek-speaking Jews elsewhere (7:35). Now they wonder whether he will commit suicide, and thus rule himself out of the age to come. The irony is that for all the Jews' ignorance, there is a grain of truth in both their questions. Jesus will eventually go to the Greeks through the Church's mission, and he will lay down his own life. But for now, the truth is hidden from those who are 'from below ... of this world'. The contrast between 'above' and 'below' should not be seen in terms of other-worldliness: the spiritual versus the material. It is a matter of 'believing that I am he' as opposed to 'dying in your sin': what the prologue calls being 'born of God' rather than 'of the will of the flesh or of man' (1:13).

Verse 24 contains the first of four absolute 'I am' statements in this Gospel: '... unless you believe that *I am*' (see also 8:28, 8:58, 13:19). This provokes the understandable response, 'Who are you?' Jesus reiterates what he has been saying since 5:18 about the continuity between his words and work and the Father who sent him. But he goes further in verse 28, by introducing the reference to 'lifting up the Son of man'. We have already met the double meaning in this expression in 3:14, and it is developed further in the passion narrative. Jesus will 'go away', not by killing himself but by allowing his enemies to take his life from him. This act of self-sacrifice will reveal his true identity. 'He who sent me is with me; he has not left me alone', because the Spirit has descended from heaven and remains on him (1:32ff). So Jesus' lifting up will prove to be the supreme instance of his oneness with his Father's will and purpose: 'God so loved the world that he gave his only Son'.

Will Jesus' passion really convince his opponents of his authority and destiny? Only if they allow themselves to be drawn into the impact of his passion on the world. How could such a humiliated and disgraced Jewish rabbi inspire such a vigorous movement if he were not from God? But as we shall see in tomorrow's reading, even those who take Jesus at his word here must struggle to stay true to him.

2 From which father? *Read John 8:31–47*

Jesus challenges those who believe in him to '*continue* in my word'. The Greek is translated elsewhere by 'remain' or 'abide', and suggests a willingness to live with Jesus' teaching so that it can liberate believers from the after-effects of unbelief. His audience are clearly not impressed by the suggestion that they need to be set free, so much so that they deny one of the main themes of their history: 'we have never been in bondage to anyone'. What about Egypt? Babylon? Rome? But they are not as free to serve God as they imagine. As 'slaves to sin' they are under the sway of unbelief, and this calls into question their right to see themselves as children of Abraham. For Jesus, unbelief is not simply a contrary opinion of his origins and authority, but a particular way of acting. If belief acknowledges the truth of Jesus' divine origin and his authority to interpret the law according to the spirit of life, unbelief shows itself in the pursuit of death: 'now you seek to kill me, a man who has told you the truth which I heard from God; this is not what Abraham did.'

'You do what your father did.' If these Jews cannot be Abraham's children, who then is their father? Notice the implied slur on Jesus' paternity in verse 41: are they suggesting that *he* was 'born of fornication'? If they are, this may be evidence of uncertainty about Jesus' family background, either among Jesus' or the evangelist's audience (but compare 6:42, which is set in Galilee). The argument now moves beyond human origins to the issue of spiritual affinity: 'we have one Father, even God'. Malachi 2:10ff is worth reading here. The prophet condemns the priesthood for corrupting God's covenant people, and appeals to the fatherhood of God: 'Have we not all one father? Has not one God created us? Why then are we faithless to one another, profaning the covenant of our fathers?' Jesus draws attention to a similarly corrupting breach of God's covenant in his own day—one which prefers death to life, slavery to freedom, and reveals a spiritual affinity with the devil rather than God. Demonizing opponents—like questioning paternity—was a standard way of impugning their honour (see Mark 3:22ff). But there is more to this argument than trading insults. Jesus maintains throughout that his origins lie in the God of life, who has sent him into the world. By contrast, these Jews who reject the truth revealed in Jesus and seek to kill him are 'of your father the devil ... a murderer from the beginning ... the father of lies'. If Jesus has been sent by God, they are on a mission from the devil.

It is worth reminding ourselves that this harsh disagreement sprang out of Jesus' healing of a paralysed man on the sabbath day (5:1–18). The reaction to his act of compassion lays bare the way in which a religious tradition—its way of believing in and worshipping and serving God—can become demonic if it resists life by sanctioning the way of violence. It would be a mistake to restrict Jesus' critique to one version of religion. All religious traditions, including those which originate from Jesus, need to come under his scrutiny.

3 Before Abraham *Read John 8:48–59*

The insults fly thick and fast as Jesus is accused of being a mad Samaritan. In his defence he makes the now familiar claim to honour his Father and seek his glory. On the day of judgment it is Jesus and those who keep his word who will be vindicated. In this sense they 'will never see death'. The Jews misunderstand, thinking that he envisages an end to physical death, which is clearly ludicrous. As they rightly insist, their great men of honour—

Abraham and the prophets—have all died. But by using 'life' as the criterion of truth, Jesus is speaking qualitatively. In this gospel 'life' means communion with God, characterized by love for the Father in the community of believers. As we shall see in the farewell discourses at the last supper, this life is stronger than death.

Jesus turns his confidence in God's vindication of him against his opponents. 'The Father glorifies me' because 'I know him and keep his word. But you do not know him.' Action provides the clue to origin. Now Jesus appeals to Abraham, but with a difference. The Jews have just used him as an example of death, but for Jesus he is on the side of life. In what sense did 'your father Abraham rejoice to see my day'? Perhaps Jesus is referring to the rabbinic belief that God gave Abraham a vision of the messianic era. Again the Jews misunderstand: 'have you seen Abraham?' (Notice that some gospel manuscripts alter this.) But Jesus turns their misunderstanding to his own advantage: if you want to know whether I have seen Abraham, then 'truly, truly I say to you, before Abraham was, I am'.

At the very least Jesus claims to have more honour than Abraham: he is 'before Abraham', in the same way that he is 'before' John the Baptist (1:15). That alone would be blasphemy, and worthy of stoning. But in the Greek Bible, 'I am' refers to God (e.g. Exodus 3:14; Isaiah 43:10). 'Before Abraham was, I am' takes us back, via the 'I am' statements in verses 24 and 28, to 5:18, where Jesus is said to be 'equal with God' in the sense that he does the Father's work and speaks the Father's word; and still further back to 'the beginning', when the Word was with God (1:1). All that Jesus has been saying between 5:18 and 8:58 about his origin and destiny, his mission and vindication, is a commentary on what is meant in this gospel by his divinity. But this is a vulnerable divinity, subject to violence. The section which begins with Jesus' declaring 'I am the light of the world' (8:12) ends with his enemies picking up stones. 'The true light … came to his own home, and his own people received him not' (1:9–10).

4 Out of the darkness *Read John 9:1–12*

'As he passed by' hardly looks like a natural sequel to Jesus' hasty escape in 8:59. The more natural connection is with 8:12, especially as this is repeated in verse 5. The disciples' question reflects traditional understandings of the links between suffering and sin. They expect a theoretical answer to the age-old problem, but Jesus provides a practical response to a concrete example of suffering. The man's blindness is neither the result of sin nor is it sent by God to give Jesus a chance to demonstrate his healing power. 'That the works of God might be made manifest in him' sees suffering as an opportunity to do God's work: 'the "work of God"... is not punishing sinners with suffering, but overcoming the suffering' (Rensberger).

The man has never been able to see. He would appreciate the feel of clay on his eyelids and the sense of liberation when he washed it off later (compare the healing of the deaf mute in Mark 7:32ff, when Jesus touched his ears, spat on his tongue and looked up to heaven). But there is a deeper meaning: if the clay symbolizes the earth from which God made the first man, then this healing is an act of creation, the work of God. And the name of the pool—'Siloam, which means Sent'—underlines Jesus' statement that he is doing 'the works of him who sent me'. According to traditional Jewish expectation, with the healing of a blind man the age of salvation has dawned (Isaiah 35:5; 42:7).

Opinion is divided (not unexpectedly) as to whether this is the formerly blind beggar, and it is left to the man himself to dispel the confusion: 'I am the man.' He tells of what has happened to him. Notice how he refers to Jesus—'the man called Jesus'—and his ignorance of Jesus' true identity is highlighted by the fact that he does not know where he is. In fact Jesus has disappeared from the story: he left in verse 7, to return in verse 35. He is absent for most of the narrative (27 of its 41 verses), making the man its main character. This suggests that his 'I do not know' will not be his last word about the man called Jesus.

5 Out of the synagogue *Read John 9:13–23*

Up to now Jesus has been on trial before the Jewish authorities. Here it is the man who is hauled before the Pharisees. They are divided. The fact that a healing has taken place on the sabbath day is enough for some of them to condemn Jesus as a sinner. Even if they are prepared to concede that healing is part of God's continuing work, they can hardly say the same for making clay. Other Pharisees, though, cannot square the idea of Jesus being a sinner with such a significant sign. So they ask the man for his opinion of Jesus. Notice the development of his understanding: 'the man called Jesus' is now 'a prophet'.

This is no help to the Pharisees, who are now united in pursuing a different strategy. If Jesus is a sinner, he cannot possibly heal a man born blind. Therefore the man was not blind in the first place. The Pharisees test their hypothesis by interrogating the man's parents, who confirm that he was born blind but deny all knowledge of how he has come to see. 'We do not know ... ask him; he is of age, he will speak for himself' looks innocent enough at first sight, but it is more sinister in the light of verse 22. By seeking to protect themselves, the man's parents in fact betray him. They leave him wide open to the malevolence of the Jewish leaders.

As far as we know, no one was expelled from the synagogue for confessing Jesus as the Christ during his lifetime. We do not know when, if ever, this became general policy. But it could well have happened locally as relationships between church and synagogue deteriorated after the fall of Jerusalem in AD70. So this incident is not likely to have been historical in the sense that it happened during the ministry of Jesus. Its historical value lies elsewhere, in what it reveals of the experience of the church for which the evangelist was writing (on this, see also the notes on chapter 3, *Guidelines* May–August 1998). The formerly blind man, the leading character in the story, represents the Johannine Christians who face such hostility from the Jewish community that they must choose between synagogue and church.

Why were relationships between the two communities so strained? Sharp disagreement over the authority of Jesus, fed by religious rivalry, would hardly promote good relations. A church attractive to Jews, offering the opportunity to mix more freely with Gentiles, could only undermine the cohesion of their community, something the Jewish leaders wanted to strengthen after AD70. In such circumstances tensions easily spill over into violence, of which the threat of expulsion is only a part.

6 In sin—in faith *Read John 9:24–41*

Once more the authorities interrogate the formerly blind man. If he represents Johannine Christians, his experience anticipates Jesus' later words to his disciples in 16:2: 'They will put you out of the synagogues; indeed the hour is coming when whoever kills you will think he is offering service to God.' The way he deals with hostility provides a model for Christians under trial.

For the Jewish leaders, Jesus must be a sinner because he flouts the sabbath law given by God to Moses. But the man uses a different criterion to assess Jesus. He takes his stand on his own experience: 'One thing I know, that though I was blind, now I see.' Such an unprecedented act of mercy can only mean one thing: 'If this man were not from God, he could do nothing.' In their anger the Jews show their disdain for the man. 'You were born in utter sin' reflects the traditional associations between suffering and sin, and at the same time reveals the extent of their confusion. Two scenes ago it suited them to insist that the man could not possibly have been born blind. Now they maintain the very opposite, because they are under no obligation to listen to one who was 'born in utter sin'. We have met contempt like this before (7:47ff).

Sin has been running through this story like a thread. If sin cannot be identified with suffering or sabbath-breaking, what does it consist of? The flowering of the man's faith demonstrates this gospel's understanding of the nature of sin as unbelief. Over the course of the narrative his spiritual sight develops. First he sees Jesus as 'a man', then 'a prophet', then one who is 'from God' and finally, as Jesus returns to the story, as 'Son of man' and 'Lord'. Jesus speaks of sight and blindness as metaphors of faith and unbelief. Who then *really* sees? Who is *truly* blind? Who is *really* a sinner? The Pharisees' condition is only aggravated by their refusal to recognize it.

GUIDELINES

The Lamb of God takes away the sin of the world by opening the eyes of faith. Jesus' mission involves him in adversity. The same is true of those whose eyes are opened. But faith can grow through adversity. As someone has said, faith is like a muscle: it grows by being stretched.

Though reassuring for Johannine believers and others whose faith is stretched, this is daunting for those who are not used to the struggle. Hence the importance of remembering the corporateness of Christian experience, not least through the fellowship of Bible reading and prayer.

Lord, strengthen those whose faith is being stretched today.
Encourage them by the examples of people like the man
whose eyes Jesus opened.
Use my/our prayers to make faith more resilient,
and to help it grow.

16–22 NOVEMBER JOHN 10:1—11:46

1 Into and out of the sheepfold *Read John 10:1–10*

At first reading, verse 1 looks like a clumsy link with the previous chapter, but 10:21 refers back to the healing of the blind man. And as the narrative progresses Jesus speaks figuratively ('figure' in verse 6 is the nearest we get in this gospel to the parables in the synoptics), developing his previous words in 9:41 to present a searing critique of the Jewish leadership.

Jesus uses a familiar image: throughout the Middle East, sheep were enclosed in the courtyard of a house. His words also set up strong biblical resonances. 'The Lord is my shepherd' (Psalm 23). The rabbis thought of Moses as Israel's shepherd. In Numbers 27:17ff, Moses is commanded to invest some of his authority in his successor Joshua, 'that the congregation of the Lord may not be as sheep which have no shepherd'. The authority of Joshua the shepherd is such that 'at his word [Israel] shall go out, and at his word they shall come in...' But Israel's shepherds often fell short of the Mosaic ideal. The prophets condemned the corrupt shepherds of Israel, and looked forward to God's coming as a shepherd in the person of the Davidic messiah (Ezekiel 34; see also Jeremiah 10; Zechariah 11).

In his interpretation of the figure, Jesus announces that the expected time has arrived, and lays claim to be the true interpreter of the authority of Moses ('Joshua' is the Hebrew equivalent of 'Jesus'). The contrast between the shepherd and the thieves could not be sharper. He knows his sheep intimately, and leads them to where they can find pasture; those who are strangers to the flock are driven only by self-interest. The shepherd's leadership brings life, the thieves' leads only to death. Surprisingly perhaps, Jesus identifies himself first with the door (v. 7). He is the boundary between sheepfold and pasture, the point of access to sustenance and life. There are echoes here of the synoptic language of 'entering' the kingdom of God, sometimes explicitly through a narrow 'gate' or 'door' (Matthew 7:13; Luke 13:24), and of Jesus' words in 1:51, where the Son of Man stands at the boundary between heaven and earth. In typical Johannine fashion, 'I am the door' exalts Jesus as the way to abundant life—the point repeatedly made in his signs and teaching. If, as we have seen already, 'life' is the key that unlocks the meaning of the law, 'life' is also the measure of true leadership. Tragically, Israel's leaders are guilty of dealing in death.

2 Laying down life, taking it again *Read John 10:11–21*

The focus of attention shifts from the door to the shepherd, who is now contrasted not with 'thieves and robbers' but with the 'hireling'. He too is motivated by self-interest. He has no real affinity with the sheep and cares nothing for them, so that when danger threatens he abandons them. By contrast the 'good shepherd' knows and is known by his sheep, and is prepared to put his life at risk for them.

When it is applied to Jesus, 'good' is more than a statement of competence or even quality. 'He is a good man', according to some people in Jerusalem (7:12), where goodness is associated with God. Jesus is 'the good shepherd' because he embodies God's shepherdly care for his people, and even for 'other sheep that are not of this fold'—like the Samaritans in chapter 4, and Gentiles who are drawn into the people of God through the mission of the church. The Jewish leaders cannot even care for their own people, let alone foreigners. Their self-interest has driven them to expel the formerly blind man from the synagogue, itself a kind of sheepfold for God's flock. They behave like hired labourers, showing their lack of concern for God's flock by abandoning one of them to the ravages of wolves. By contrast Jesus went to find him, like a genuine shepherd searching for a lost sheep (9:34–35).

Jesus' life has been increasingly under threat since 5:18. Now for the first time he speaks openly and clearly of his death—four times in these verses (vv. 11, 15, 17, 18). The imagery of 'laying down life … taking it again' recalls the gospel's 'descent–ascent' motif. Heaven and earth meet in Jesus' willingness to *give* his life: not even his enemies will take it from him. 'Laying down ... taking it again' underlines the Johannine belief that the movement which culminates in the passion of the *good* shepherd is entirely from God: 'God so loved the world that he gave his only Son.' Notice that Jesus' sacrifice brings together his care for and knowledge of the sheep, and God's love for and knowledge of him. There is a perfect continuity between God's shepherdly care for his flock and Jesus' willingness to lay down his life, which gives him the authority to 'take it again'. In his dying and rising, as in his healing, Jesus makes himself equal with God (cf. 5:18). Divine love, made flesh in Jesus, works through its vulnerability. This is where its real power lies. And this is why many accuse Jesus of being mad. To worship a vulnerable God is to embrace vulnerability oneself—not something for which leaders are noted.

3 In the flock, and outside it *Read John 10:22–39*

The narrative now jumps forward two months, from Tabernacles to the December Feast of Dedication (Hanukkah), which celebrated the purification of the temple in 165BC after it was desecrated by the foreign ruler, Antiochus Epiphanes.

Jesus' figure of the sheepfold was full of messianic allusions, but even the force of his 'I am the door' and 'I am the good shepherd' has made no impression on these Jews: 'If you are the Christ, tell us plainly.' The problem is one of hearing rather than explanation: communication is, after all, a two-way process. Rather than going over the same ground yet again, Jesus now applies the figure to his audience. If they really belonged to God's flock, they would have no difficulty believing his message. But they cannot 'see' who he is because their self-interest has blinded them (9:40f). The contrast between those in the flock and those outside it could not be more stark. Jesus' own sheep are safe: the words in verses 28 and 29 would certainly have provided welcome 'pasture' for hard-pressed Johannine believers.

'I and the Father are one' in the exercise of divine, shepherdly care for the flock. If the Jews find this offensive they need to remember the text in which God addresses Israel: 'You are gods, sons of the Most High' (Psalm 82:6). The rabbis believed that this referred to the giving of the Law, which made people divine in the sense that the angel of death had no power over them. If the Law can achieve this, why is it so difficult for the Jewish leaders to recognize the divinity of Jesus? They are celebrating the dedication of the temple (and presumably also of themselves) to God. But Jesus shows what it means to be truly consecrated to God's will (v. 36): true dedication—true divinity—is seen in what he reveals of the power of life over death. So Jesus presses his claim that his life-giving acts of healing should be seen as signs of his divine authority: 'Believe the works, that you may know and understand that the Father is in me and I am in the Father.'

Blasphemy is a political as well as a religious charge: in Jesus' day these two dimensions were inseparable. The Jewish leaders in Jerusalem believed that they taught with God's authority. Throughout his 'trial' in Jerusalem (this scene summarizes the arguments we have heard since 5:19), Jesus has rejected their claim, and exposed the self-interest masked by their honour and power. He and the authorities are on a collision course, and this is the last time that he will escape their clutches.

4 Across the Jordan, then to Bethany *Read John 10:40—11:16*

The tension mounts. It is only a matter of time before the repeated attempts on Jesus' life will prove successful. He has indicated as much by speaking openly about laying down his own life. For the moment he seeks refuge across the Jordan 'where John at first baptized'. This reminds us of the baptizer's testimony to Jesus early in the gospel (see 1:26ff; 3:27ff). However the Jewish authorities see him, Jesus is the messiah who baptizes with the Spirit of life, the Lamb of God whose passion removes the sin of unbelief and opens the eyes of faith. The following story bears out the truth of John's witness.

The way in which the narrative points backwards and forwards shows that we have reached a significant moment in the gospel. The naming of Lazarus, Martha and Mary, and the description of Lazarus as 'he whom you love', suggests that they belong to Jesus' flock (10:3): 'I give (my sheep) eternal life and they shall never perish' (10:28) leads us to expect great things of Jesus here. The mention of Bethany and Jesus' anointing by Mary anticipate the passion narrative (12:1ff). There are echoes of the healing of the man born blind. Verse 4 reminds us of 9:3ff: here is another opportunity to respond to human suffering by doing God's work. Verses 9 and 10 recall 9:4f. That Lazarus' illness 'is for the glory of God' links it with Jesus' death and resurrection, where the Son of God is glorified (chapter 17). The threat to Jesus and the disciples harks back to the previous chapter (and to the earlier attempts on his life). The irony in Thomas' bemused response to Jesus' decision in verse 16 is apparent by the time we reach the sayings about discipleship in 12:23ff.

The significance of this story is only heightened by the way time slows down as the narrative progresses: about four days elapse between verses 1 and 17, but verses 17–44 occupy the same day. This mirrors the passage of time in the gospel as a whole: chapters 1–12 cover two years or more (three Passovers—2:23, 6:4, 12:1); chapters 13–21 span a matter of weeks. It is as if the evangelist is saying to his readers, 'This story—the last of Jesus' signs—captures the meaning of the whole gospel.' As sleep is a metaphor for death (vv. 11ff), so the raising of Lazarus is a parable of the life-giving power of Jesus which culminates in his passion and resurrection. There is only one reason for telling the story—'so that you may believe' (v. 15). But what are the benefits of this faith?

5 To Martha *Read John 11:17–27*

Jesus waited two days before deciding to cross the Jordan again and go to Bethany (v. 6). The delay is understandable in view of the danger he faced; but in the end it didn't matter. It would have taken a day for the sisters' message to reach Jesus, and a day for him to travel to Bethany. By the time he arrived, Lazarus had been dead for four days. This suggests that he was already dead by the time Jesus heard about his illness.

Martha reacts to Jesus with a mixture of disappointment and confidence. If only he had been able to reach Lazarus sooner... but now that he is here, he can at least bring some consolation from God. It is clear from her words in verse 24 that she is not expecting Jesus to raise Lazarus from the sleep of death. She shares the (by now) traditional Jewish belief that on the day of resurrection, 'those who sleep in the dust of the earth shall be raised to... everlasting life' (Daniel 12:2). So she is comforted by Jesus' reassuring words: 'Your brother will rise again.' But like Thomas earlier in the story, she misses Jesus' meaning: he has come to wake Lazarus out of his sleep (v. 11).

'I am the resurrection and the life' is another example of the way this gospel transfers elements of Jewish hope for a future day of salvation to the present, and makes Jesus the one in whom hope is realized (cf. 'I am the bread of life'; see the notes on chapter 6). Faith in him brings 'the resurrection at the last day'—one of the Jewish symbols of the coming salvation of the world—into the present moment. Martha's confession gathers up the responses of all those in the gospel—John the baptizer, Andrew, Philip, Nathaniel, the Samaritan woman, the official at Cana, Peter, the man born blind—who have recognized the life-giving power of Jesus as the one sent by God to redeem the world. Jews in the Johannine church who, like the man born blind, had been ostracized from the synagogue, would certainly benefit from Martha's faith in Jesus. He fulfils the traditional hopes for a new world: the future promised by God takes shape around him. And its essential quality is the life that overcomes every form of death.

6 To the place of death *Read John 11:28–46*

Martha the confessor becomes Martha the witness, as she calls her sister Mary to come to Jesus. Referring to him as 'the Teacher' implies a measure of trust in what he has been saying. Understandably Martha wants Mary to share the benefits of her faith in Jesus. It is unwise to read too much into the descriptions of the sisters' emotional states, but on the face of it Mary seems the more distressed. Too upset, perhaps, at first to leave the house with

Martha and meet Jesus, she gives every indication to her consolers that she would rather weep than speak. When she eventually meets Jesus she expresses Martha's initial disappointment without any of her confidence.

Jesus is deeply affected by the grief he encounters: his response is mentioned three times (vv. 33, 35, 38). Typically he divides opinion among the mourning Jews. Some see him grieving out of love for Lazarus; others wonder whether he is weeping for his own failure. He can hardly be grieving for Lazarus or himself if he knows that he has come to wake his dear friend out of his sleep. It is more likely that Jesus is reacting to the impact of death on a family and a community. He grieves here not for himself but for others. He reveals his ability to enter into sorrow where it is most deeply felt. The image of the grieving Jesus is worth cherishing, not least because this gospel can give the impression that Jesus' divinity is always at the expense of his humanity. Yet it is surely here, in the grief that expresses his vulnerability—his readiness to be affected by the world God loves—that his humanity reveals the true nature of divinity.

At the tomb, which anticipates his own, Jesus stands on the boundary of life and death. Brushing aside Martha's hesitation at his request to open up the tomb, he reiterates his promise to flood the present moment with God's future glory. He justifies her earlier confidence in him (v. 22), but not without declaring his own confidence in his Father, in the hope that the crowd will also come to share Martha's faith. Many—but ominously, not all—of them do when they see Lazarus emerging from the tomb, bearing witness to the life-giving power of Jesus' word (cf 4:43ff; 5:25, 28).

What are we to make of this account? It is worth remembering that Lazarus eventually returned to his grave: his raising is but a foretaste of 'the resurrection at the last day'. However we explain it, the story is at least a parable which shows the power of God to overcome death by life, where 'death' is represented by unbelief and sorrow as well as mortality, and 'life' by faith in Jesus the Christ. As we leave the story, we should not allow ourselves to lose sight of Jesus' grief among the mourners. This messiah does not ride roughshod over the world's sorrows. He can only save the world by entering into its agonies and letting himself be touched by them. Lazarus and the others in Jesus' flock are only fully and finally redeemed by the good shepherd's laying down his life for them. This is the work of God: 'I and the Father are one.'

GUIDELINES

Christianity is sometimes criticized for its images of God's power. 'King' and 'Lord', for example, are rooted in ages when men wielded power which often relied on brutality and violence. 'High' Christology has often taken on aspects of these understandings of power: men have fought wars, conquered new worlds and demanded subservience in the name of this kind of Christ.

The story of the raising of Lazarus, with its unforgettable image of Jesus weeping by the tomb, presents a different picture of God. This vulnerability is part of the story of the self-expression of God in human experience, the Word made flesh.

The highest Christology is that which sees such solidarity between God and the world—in its sorrows as well as its joys—that he is utterly vulnerable.

God of Jesus, your strength lies in your ability
to take the world's suffering into yourself
without being diminished by it.
Open our eyes to your life-giving power.

23–29 NOVEMBER JOHN 11:45—12:50

1 To the Pharisees and the ruling council *Read John 11:45–54*

Popular disaffection with Jesus now contributes directly to the authorities' decision to have him executed. The 'council' is the Jewish ruling body, the Sanhedrin, to which the Roman imperial powers had delegated the authority to run Judea. Caiaphas, the high priest, was a political appointee. He and his class did well out out of compromising with Rome. They maintained their interests in the temple, which was a centre of trade and banking as well as religion, while the Romans maintained their practice of ruling through local officials. Among the principal responsibilities of the Jewish leaders was collecting the taxes levied by Rome; another was keeping the peace. When civil disturbances broke out among the Jews, the Romans had a reputation for heavy-handed intervention. Wise leaders knew that they only held on to their power by suppressing dissent.

This explains why the Jewish council finally decides to act against Jesus. The raising of Lazarus has made Jesus more popular than ever. The prospect of his popularity continuing to grow is unthinkable. A man who draws large crowds can easily undermine the public order on which the council's authority relies, and never more so than at festivals, when Jerusalem is full of pilgrims celebrating God's liberating deeds in the past. Not only the holy place, but the whole nation is at risk: direct rule from Rome is less desirable than the current arrangements. The Romans used crucifixion as a way of controlling their subjects. To allow 'one man to die for the people' would not only remove a dangerous irritant, it would also deter other potential troublemakers, and so maintain the delicate balance of power in Judea. This account also sheds important historical light on the synoptic version of the trial of Jesus. We gain the impression that the decision to have Jesus executed was made before his arrest. His subsequent interrogation by the Sanhedrin was not so much a legal trial as an opportunity to ratify the decision that had already been made to have Jesus handed over to the Roman governor for execution.

The passage is shot through with irony. The decision to have Jesus executed is forced by the raising of Lazarus. The high priest's political expediency fulfils the words of the good shepherd, who lays down his life for the sheep in the 'one flock' (10:16). 'The children of God who are scattered abroad' includes Jews dispersed throughout the known world, from whom the early Christianity drew many of its members. But there is also a strong hint that Jesus' passion will bear fruit in mission to the Gentiles.

Despite the powers acting against him, Jesus still controls his destiny. He remains on the edges of the wilderness until he is ready to act. However expedient it may be to kill him, his life will be given, not taken.

2 From Ephraim to Bethany *Read John 11:55—12:11*

'The Passover of the Jews' sounds a significant chord in the narrative. The ritual killing of lambs recalls the Lamb of God who takes away the sin of the world (1:29). The recent raising of Lazarus reminds us of an earlier Passover when people were drawn to Jesus by signs, but he regarded their faith as inadequate (2:23ff). Passover was also at hand when Jesus spoke of himself as the bread of life: 'The bread which I shall give for the life of the world is my flesh' (6:51). Will he or won't he come? Last time people wondered about Jesus' presence at a festival, he came in private (7:10). But not this time, as we shall see.

Bethany has Jesus among friends again. Matthew and Mark also have Jesus anointed in Bethany, but at the house of Simon the leper, where an unnamed woman pours expensive oil over his head and the disciples complain about the waste (Mark 14:3ff). John's account reminds us of the anonymous woman in Luke who anoints Jesus' feet with ointment and wipes them with her hair (Luke 7:37ff). Whatever the reasons for the similarities and differences, John's account is carefully written. It points backwards and forwards: to the raising of Lazarus (in 11:32 Mary fell at Jesus' feet); to the footwashing at the last supper (13:1ff); to the burial of Jesus (in 19:38ff he is anointed by Joseph and Nicodemus). In Judas the narrative points both ways at once. As a thief he is like those who enter the sheepfold another way (10:1); as the betrayer he will break the sacred bonds of table fellowship at the supper (13:21ff).

The contrast between Judas and Mary is striking and poignant. About him there is the stench of hypocrisy, mean-spiritedness, self-interest. She releases the fragrance of genuine care, generosity, self-giving. Like her sister who serves, she is a true disciple. Some have suggested that Lazarus whom Jesus loved (11:3, 5), who was *at table* with Jesus, is the beloved disciple who *lay close* to Jesus' breast at the last supper (13:23)—the words in italics translate the same Greek word. We cannot be certain, but as they are drawn into the danger zone around Jesus, Lazarus and his sisters epitomize what he will say about the essence of discipleship in 12:26 and at the last supper.

3 Into Jerusalem *Read John 12:12–19*

As in the synoptics, Jesus enters Jerusalem at Passover-tide for the last time riding a donkey. But there are differences in detail which bring out what John sees in the event.

- **The ass:** In the other gospels Jesus sends his disciples to procure the ass. Here he is less deliberate, more spontaneous; he rides it to quell the enthusiasm of crowds excited by the raising of Lazarus (which is only recorded in John).
- **The biblical quotation:** Only here and in Matthew 21:9 is Zechariah 9:9 quoted (Matthew's version is longer). Mark and Luke simply allude to the text.
- **Palm branches:** In the synoptics, but not here, the crowds spread their clothes on the road as a mark of respect for Jesus. John alone has the crowds carrying *palm* branches. Luke does not mention any branches, while Matthew and Mark have the crowds spreading them on the road. The Maccabean stories of the purification of the Temple in 167BCE and its cleansing in 141BCE may have influenced the gospel narratives. On both occasions palm branches were carried in celebration (see 2 Maccabees 10:6–7; 1 Maccabees 13:51).
- **Acclamations:** The crowds' 'Hosanna' ('save us') and 'Blessed is he who comes in the name of the Lord' are taken from Psalm 118:25–26, which was sung in procession at the Jewish festivals and expressed well the nationalistic feelings of the pilgrims. The additional reference to Jesus as 'King of Israel' again looks backwards and forwards: to Nathaniel's confession in 1:49; to the crowds who want to make Jesus king in 6:15; to his interrogation by Pilate in 18:33ff; and to his crucifixion as 'king of the Jews' in 19:19ff. As with the cleansing of the temple (2:17, 22), only hindsight enabled the disciples to realize the significance of Jesus' action: it symbolized the liberating power of one who is a king, but not a king.

The Pharisees see enough to confirm the council's earlier decision to find some way of putting Jesus to death. 'The world has gone after him' is an overstatement born of anxiety, exasperation and perhaps jealousy: but the evangelist sees the deeper truth. Jews from all over the known world were in Jerusalem for Passover. A cosmopolitan crowd meeting and acclaiming Jesus represented the community of Jews and Gentiles in the Johannine church for whom Jesus is, as the Samaritans confessed in 4:42, the saviour of the world.

4 Into the earth *Read John 12:20–26*

The 'Greeks' here are probably Greek-speaking Jews who live outside Palestine. In wanting to 'see' Jesus, they clearly want to make a journey of discipleship: chapter 9 has taught us about sight as a metaphor for faith. The mention of Philip from Bethsaida and Andrew reminds us of their journey of discipleship in 1:35ff, when Jesus invited Andrew to 'come and see', and Philip did the same to Nathaniel. They are effective missionaries who bring others to Jesus, and are wisely sought out by the Greeks.

Jesus speaks of death, sacrifice and service as the texture of discipleship. It is necessary to talk this way because 'the hour has come for the Son of man to be glorified': his own death has been increasingly imminent since chapter 10. We have heard about 'the hour' ever since Mary's request at the wedding in Cana (2:5). Now we see that its 'not yet' is about to expire. To 'see' Jesus is to share his hour with him. This is not to wallow in tragedy or seek suffering for its own sake. The hour brings glorification for Jesus—that is, his return to the glory of heaven. So those who follow Jesus into his hour are in some sense with him in his heavenly life (v. 26; cf 14:2ff). Just as the seed has to be buried in the earth before anything grows from it, so Jesus' death will bear fruit in eternal life for those who follow his example of costly service.

'Hating life' smacks to us of despising oneself, of the low self-esteem that destroys personal and social well-being. Here, though, it means the opposite of the self-enclosed, self-absorbed life symbolized by the solitary seed, of which Jesus' enemies among the Jewish authorities are instructive examples in this gospel. 'He who hates his life in this world' allows the protective outer shell to be opened up, so that life may be laid down, given away, shared, in the fashion of Jesus.

5 Lifted up from the earth *Read John 12:27–36a*

In 11:33 Jesus was troubled by the reactions to Lazarus' death; here he is similarly troubled at the prospect of his own. John's Gospel contains no narrative of Jesus' agony in the Garden of Gethsemane: some scholars believe that this passage is the Johannine equivalent. 'Father, save me from this hour' corresponds to 'let this cup pass from me'. And 'No, for this purpose I have come to this hour. Father, glorify thy name' expresses the sentiments of 'nevertheless, not my will but your will be done' (see Mark 14:36 and parallels). After the calm control with which Jesus has so far approached his death, and the unruffled way in which he speaks of laying down his life for the sheep in 10:15ff, it comes as something of a relief to know that the Johannine Jesus finds the thought of a violent death harrowing.

Nevertheless, he does not shrink from it. In the other gospels he believes that God will ultimately vindicate him, despite his rejection by the leaders of his own people and the shame of crucifixion. Here God's vindication sounds out from heaven as Jesus speaks. Only at this point in the gospel is the heavenly voice mentioned (there is no voice at the baptism of Jesus, and there is no account of the transfiguration—stories in which the heavenly voice is heard in the synoptic gospels). Again the crowd are divided: is it thunder, or an angel? The purpose of 'this voice' is not to reassure Jesus as he faces death, but to convince his audience that he speaks with God's authority. His execution will make it look as if his work has ended in god-forsakenness and disgrace. But he sees it as God's 'now', the turning point of history. The lifting up of the Son of man brings heaven and earth together (1:51). The hour of crucifixion is the day of judgment, which reveals God's victory over the worst kinds of evil that people can inflict on one another—cruelty, violence, murder. The hour of suffering is also the day of salvation: through it God creates a single flock (10:16), a new humanity which honours Jesus as the one whom God has 'lifted up from the earth' to himself.

The crowd find the idea of a dying messiah unacceptable. This is not surprising, as it is not found in contemporary Jewish writings. 'Who is this Son of man?' is the formerly blind man's question in 9:36. Jesus can only answer in metaphors of light and darkness. 'While you have the light' is an invitation to believe while there is still time, but also a warning that the shadows are lengthening fast.

6 Into hiding *Read John 12:36b–50*

Jesus' public ministry ends on this dramatic note. The evangelist reflects on the significance of the story we have been reading. An abundance of signs has not managed to point Jesus' Jewish audience towards faith. Even those of the authorities who do believe in him cannot bring themselves to confess their faith openly and publicly. The social cost is too great (see the notes on Nicodemus in chapter 3, *Guidelines* May–August 1998). It is as if the experience of an earlier preacher in Jerusalem, the prophet Isaiah, has been repeated. 'The arm of the Lord' (an image of God's saving power) has certainly been revealed to the people of Jerusalem, but 'who has believed our report?' Verse 40 suggests that the responsibility lies with God, who has 'blinded their eyes and hardened their heart'. This is a Semitic way of saying that all that has happened lies within the providence of God, who will use even the rejection of his Son for his good purposes.

The evangelist allows Jesus to have the last word: he speaks from his hiding place, as if addressing an audience looking at an empty and darkened stage. If the evangelist has given us his reflections in verses 37–43, it is now Jesus' turn to offer his. Notice how his words recapture the leading themes of the first twelve chapters: faith, the one sent by God, light and darkness, salvation and judgment, divine authority and eternal life. Echoes of chapter 1 give a sense of ending (see especially 1:4–9): these verses are the epilogue, as 1:1–18 are the prologue, to Jesus' public ministry. From here on in the gospel, Jesus' words are reserved for the inner circle of his followers, as he prepares them for the hour of his departure.

GUIDELINES

Talk of Jesus' death is inseparable from the call to discipleship. The idea of sacrificing ourselves is not popular in contemporary Western society, even in our churches. We are rightly suspicious of anything that encourages people to be treated as doormats or abused.

The sacrifice of Christian discipleship is Christ-shaped. Vulnerable as he was, this gospel insists that Jesus did not allow his life to be taken from him: he gave it freely, out of love for his Father and his flock. Sacrifice is not at the expense of freedom: we are called by the one 'in knowledge of whom standeth our eternal life, whose service is perfect freedom' (*Book of Common Prayer*).

Guard us, Lord, from any idea of sacrifice
that robs human beings of their dignity.
Renew our vision of the freely offered life of Christ,
and let it shape everything that calls itself by his name.

Further reading

Kenneth Grayston, *The Gospel of John*, Epworth Press 1990, is an accessible and reasonably-priced commentary on the English text.

C.K. Barrett, *The Gospel According to St John*, Second Edition, SPCK 1978, is a richly rewarding commentary on the Greek text.

Mark Stibbe, *John. Readings: A New Biblical Commentary*, JSOT Press 1993, takes a literary approach.

David Rensberger, *Overcoming The World. Politics and Community in the Gospel of John*, SPCK 1988, is a readable collection of essays with a sociological approach.

Lamentations

Lamentations comprises five separate poems which grieve over the fall of Jerusalem and the destruction of its temple in 587BC. Each poem has 22 verses (in chapter 3 they are set out as 66, but the length of the poem is the same as that of chapters 1 or 2). This corresponds to the number of letters in the Hebrew alphabet, and in chapters 1–4 each verse begins with a different letter. The poems thus express grief from A to Z. Chapters 1–3 do not begin as prayers (they are not addressed to God) but they become prayers before the end. Chapter 4 is at no point explicit prayer; chapter 5 is prayer from the beginning. Chapters 1–2 and 4 are actually more like funeral laments: they are mourning the death of a city.

The poems have the two formal features of Hebrew poetry, parallelism and rhythm. Their parallelism means that lines usually divide into two halves; the second half restates or takes further or completes or contrasts with the first half. You can see different ways in which they do this if you look at each of the three lines of the first six verses of Lamentations 1. The first line of verse 7 then breaks the pattern; there are other 'rogue' lines through the book, but in general these poems are more regular than ones in the Psalms or the Prophets.

Their rhythm is also more consistent than other Hebrew poetry. Outside Lamentations, the most common rhythm involves each half of a line containing three important words and thus three stresses. The second most common rhythm involves three stresses in the first half but only two in the second, and this is how Lamentations works. The 3–2 rhythm is used for more lyrical poetry, especially for the expression of hurt. The effect is that the second half of the line always brings you up short—you expect it to be longer than it is. It feels incomplete—which is how life is, at the moment. You can generally see even from an English translation that the second half-lines in Lamentations look shorter than the first.

1 Miss Zion overthrown *Read Lamentations 1:1–13*

The first poem makes more than do any others of the personification of Jerusalem as a woman. In other cultures a goddess such as Athene represented her city in heaven. In Israel that idea is demythologized. Yahweh does have a consort, but the consort is the city itself, bedecked with her jewels and crowned by her walls. In the case of Jerusalem, however, the wife has now become like a widow, the queen like a slave, the beloved friendless, the splendid humiliated, the honoured despised, the protected invaded. In the phrase 'daughter of Zion' the 'of' is like that in a phrase such as 'City of London': it means 'Daughter Zion', 'Miss Zion'.

According to the previous page of the Old Testament (Jeremiah 52:28–30), the number of people who have actually been deported from the city is smaller than the poem might seem to imply. Poetic hyperbole is involved, but the language also reflects the fact that all the important people were taken—government, civil service, priesthood, and skilled workers. That would of course be enough to paralyse the city. Those who mourned its fate would be ordinary people such as farmers, whom the Babylonians intended to leave behind, and other leaders who escaped deportation.

In the Psalms, a lament of this kind would usually include a protest that the reversal which the city has experienced is unjustified; the community has done nothing to deserve the devastation it has experienced. In contrast to that, in Lamentations the poet invites the people to accept their calamity as the deserved outcome of their wrongdoing. In English Bibles, Lamentations follows Jeremiah, in deference to the tradition that Jeremiah was their author. There is no historical basis to the tradition, but the poems do take the kind of view that Jeremiah would have taken, that the city has done wrong and is stained by its wrong. In Old Testament thinking (as in our experience), it takes time for a stain to disappear.

The recurrence of the statement that Miss Zion has no comforter (vv. 2, 9; also 16, 17, 21) is noteworthy, because it forms the background to the proclamation in Isaiah 40:1, 'Comfort, comfort my people, says your God.'

2 The angry God *Read Lamentations 2:1–15*

The anger of Israel's God is a prominent motif in the second poem. It is the reason why wrongdoing issued in disaster. In Hebrew the word most commonly rendered 'anger' is also a word for the nose or face, so it suggests the feelings expressed in an angry look or an angry snort. The 'wrath' of verse 2 suggests something that overflows, the bursting out of temper. The fierceness of verse 3 and the wrath of verse 4 are words which suggest white-hot burning rage; hence its being likened to fire in both verses. The fierceness of verse 6 suggests the indignation of someone who feels they have been treated with gross inappropriateness.

Two realities underlie this bold talk of Yahweh's anger. One is the experience of being on the receiving end of it. We know when someone has lashed out at us in fury; we have felt the results. Miss Zion was not starting from theological theory in speaking of Yahweh being angry with her, but from what had happened. The other reality is the typical Israelite conviction that Yahweh is a person, with all a person's passion. In a paradoxical way the bad news of Yahweh's fierce indignation which issues in snorting temper and overflows in burning rage undergirds the good news that Yahweh has the other passions of love and compassion.

This second poem expresses the human horror of what had happened to Jerusalem: see, for example, verses 11–12. We may feel that this horror exceeded the destruction of its buildings and the loss of its honour. But the dagger that pierced to the city's heart was also the disproving of the vision which it believed God had given it. We have noted that Isaiah 40 will in due course look back to Lamentations 1. Lamentations 2:15 itself looks back to confessions of faith such as Psalm 48:2. They have been discredited. In reality there were few people who happened to walk past Jerusalem (v. 15). Jerusalem is not on a main road. The questioners of verse 15 are the externalization of the city's own people. The city's fall has raised yet-unanswered questions about their own beliefs.

3 Is there still hope? *Read Lamentations 3:1, 16–30*

After the focus on Miss Zion, the 'I am the man' of verse 1 is a surprise. Lamentations 3 is especially reminiscent of the laments in the Psalter, the laments of Jeremiah, or the portrait of Yahweh's servant in Isaiah 53, though this man continues to talk *about* Yahweh rather than to speak *to* Yahweh.

In the Psalms, affliction can be described from three angles: it is what I experience, what my enemy has brought about, and what you (Yahweh) have done or not done. Here the first-person experience recurs, but the third- and second-person verbs frighteningly merge. The enemy who attacks is the Yahweh who is usually addressed, and there is therefore no one whom it is realistic to address. Splendour is not the only thing that has gone: so has hope (vv. 16–18).

If this were Jeremiah 20 or Psalm 88, that might be an end, and the bulk of verses 19–21 would only make the hopelessness deeper. In the Psalms, again, 'remembering' is a resource: remembering Yahweh's past faithfulness may feel poignant in the present, but it can encourage. Lamentations 3 remembers not Yahweh's past faithfulness but the poet's pain.

The reversal in the final word of verse 21 therefore astonishes. The poet turns out to be one who has indeed looked hurt and loss steadfastly in the face, but then (in the manner of Psalm 22) refused to let it have the last word. If the recognition of wrongdoing in chapters 1 and 2 is meant, one thing it does is assert an ongoing conviction that the universe runs in a meaningful way. Calamity is not meaningless, and if Yahweh is passionately angry, this is not because of a mere fickle temper. Alongside the passion of anger is, indeed:

- *Yahweh's commitment (that which initiates or maintains a relationship against all odds)*
- *Yahweh's compassion (like the feelings of a mother for her child)*
- *Yahweh's faithfulness (a consistency which does unfailingly keep its word)*
- *Yahweh's goodness (like the goodness of the world when it was created)* (vv. 22–25)

So expectancy, seeking, hope, and acceptance are possible (vv. 26–30).

4 What comes from Yahweh's heart and from ours

Read Lamentations 3:31–42

Isaiah has already used all Lamentations' words for anger but has then added that acting in anger is Yahweh's 'strange work'; it is 'alien' to Yahweh's true nature (Isaiah 28:21). Lamentations' way of making the point is to affirm that Yahweh acts both in anger and in compassion, but to declare that the former, the casting off and bringing grief and afflicting, are things Yahweh does 'unwillingly' (v. 33). Literally, they do not come from Yahweh's heart or mind or inner being. They are not what Yahweh is like inside. This statement occurs in the line which brings us to the very centre of the central poem of the five which make up the book.

By implication, such a conviction is grounds for the exhortation to repentance that follows. Such repentance has a number of features. It involves:

- *searching out and willingly exposing things that we know we have hidden, from ourselves as much as from others (v. 40a)*
- *turning away from one person (or from persons such as other deities) to another: the most common Hebrew word for repentance is one which literally means 'turn' and thus draws attention to its being a matter of action, not merely feeling (v. 40b)*
- *reaching out to God with mind (so this is not a mere outward gesture or pretence) and hands (so this is public as well as private: it involves the whole person) (v. 41)*

It also involves a verbal owning of what we have done. This week I have been to see the film *One Fine Day*. Among many neat moments, one scene has one of the couple who are on their way to falling in love forcing the other actually to utter the words, 'I cannot manage on my own'. These words are hard to say, and are withdrawn as soon as uttered. For some of us words can be cheap, for others they can be very expensive.

Here the words are (more literally) 'we ourselves really have rebelled' (v. 42a). The poet uses two different words for 'rebel' to emphasize the point: even one of these words on its own would express one of Hebrew's strongest ways of thinking of wrongdoing.

It indicates that we personally take responsibility for our active repudiation of our commitment to Yahweh.

5 Failed promises to city and king *Read Lamentations 4:12–22*

The arrangement of Lamentations as a whole is more circular than linear. We have seen that the centre of chapter 3 expresses its highpoints of theology and spirituality. For much of the latter part of the book we revert to pained (and more concrete) descriptions of the reduction of the city.

The challenge to faith is expressed in a new way. The city was supposed to be not merely an object of beauty and a reason for joy (2:15) but an impregnable fortress (4:12). As an architectural masterpiece it was actually less remarkable than other cities of the ancient world, but as a fortress it had some claim. The Jebusites had located it on an easily defensible, rocky spur, and David knew what he was doing in making it his own capital. More significant for its strength, however, was the fact that Yahweh had made a commitment to it, promising to make it a resting place and throne 'for ever' (Psalm 132:14). Once more, the real problem lying behind verse 12 is not the confounding of the beliefs of foreigners but the confounding of Israel's own faith.

Parallel to Yahweh's commitment to Zion in Psalm 132 is Yahweh's commitment to David and his successors as the anointed kings of Jerusalem. In owning that people's hopes in this promise have been disappointed, the poet at last makes the disappointment their own rather than projecting it on to others: 'We thought…' (v. 20).

In due course the city of Jerusalem will be rebuilt, but the city will never again be enough of a magnet to bring all its sons and daughters back. In due course Davidic princes will again aspire to its throne, but prophets will be able to picture the unimaginable in envisioning a perfectly satisfactory future without kings. There are limits to the vision that can be attached to a city or a dynastic line. After President Kennedy's death, one of his supporters said, 'We will laugh again, but we will not be young again.' Jerusalem will laugh again, but it will not be young again.

Conversely the final verses of chapter 4 have to confront the insight in Lamentations 3:33 regarding priorities within Yahweh's nature. That statement spoke of what was in God's heart for human beings in general; it did not overtly confine itself to Israel. So it applies to Edom, too.

6 The unique and the repeated *Read Lamentations 5:1–22*

I have been asked why the five poems in Lamentations were not included in the Psalter. If they had been so included, I doubt whether we would have thought them out of place. I suspect that they were kept separate because they were used on their own in Israel's worship. In the Hebrew Old Testament they are one of the 'Five Scrolls', with Ruth, Song of Songs, Ecclesiastes, and Esther. Each of these scrolls is used at a particular occasion in the Jewish year. Thus, even today, Lamentations is used on the Ninth of Av, in July–August, in commemorating the fall of Jerusalem in 587BC and in AD70. There were already such solemn commemorations in the sixth century BC (see Zechariah 7:3, 5) and it would not be surprising if these poems were used on such occasions. Whereas the Psalms have been preserved in such a way as to exclude any indication of particular events which might have stimulated their prayers and praises, the poems in Lamentations have been preserved in such a way as explicitly to commemorate the event of the fall of Jerusalem.

Yet this final lament brings the five to a close in a way which most recalls the Psalms. Lamentations 5 would be quite in place in the Psalter. The threefold grief to which we referred in connection with 3:1–30 appears here in full. The specific appeals are those of the Psalms: remember, look, restore, renew. The theological assertion is that of the Psalms (see v. 19). The question is that of the Psalms (see v. 20). The fear is that of the Psalms (see v. 22). The boldness of coming to such a negative close or non-close is that of the Psalms (compare Psalm 88).

In connection with Lamentations 4 we said that Lamentations was circular rather than linear. This turns out to have been an over-simplification. The effect of the final poem is to take us to the end of a journey from the specificity of the dreadful experience through which people have gone as Jerusalem fell, to the recognition that this fits within the experience that the people have had through the centuries, and that has continued to be Jerusalem's experience. This is a kind of further grief, but a kind of reassurance and comfort.

GUIDELINES

These poems/prayers are designed to express the pain, loss, grief, uncertainty, hopelessness, hope, repentance, longing, trust, at-a-loss-ness, and anxiety of a community that has gone through disaster. If you belong to a church or a city or a society that has had that experience, then they are for you to identify with. If not, then put yourself into the position of such a community, perhaps one you are acquainted with or one you know of from the television news, perhaps Jerusalem itself, and read these poems for it.

Further reading

R. Davidson, *Jeremiah Volume II with Lamentations: Daily Study Bible*, St Andrew Press 1985.

W.J. Fuerst, *The Books of Ruth, Esther, Ecclesiastes, the Songs of Solomon, Lamentations: Cambridge Bible*, Cambridge University Press 1975.

R.B. Salters, *Jonah and Lamentations: JSOT Study Guides*, Sheffield Academic Press 1994.

The Letters of John

The Mediterranean world of the first century was a single political unit, under the Roman Empire. The Greek language was common and widespread, so people and ideas could travel rapidly and mix easily. Christianity took advantage of this freedom, and quickly established itself in many centres far away from its origins in Palestine. There was, however, another side to the coin, for these new churches were quite vulnerable. Other religious options were available for people to follow, and there was no very long tradition to guide the churches. Communications were poor, some fellowships were small and scattered, and individual leaders might have to carry a lot of responsibility in isolated congregations.

There were many travelling preachers, some of them widely known, who built up existing churches, as well as starting new ones. Some leaders worked hard to maintain contact with the churches they had founded: when you cannot meet face to face, then offering encouragement and teaching by letter is a good second best. So we have epistles in the New Testament, about twenty in all. Often these address pressures and difficulties, and offer guidance that will restrain careless conduct, or prevent people's ideas about the faith becoming unbalanced or distorted. The apostles, who had been with Jesus, had an especially important role in helping the church to remain true to its roots.

The three short letters of John carry no postmark. Possibly they were written near Ephesus, western Turkey as it now is, towards the end of the first century. However, the best introduction we have to the times and troubles which brought these letters into being is in the letters themselves. No one knows whether the three were all written at once, but they certainly have some similar perspectives. Indeed the number of words, phrases and emphases in common suggests that one author wrote all three. We shall read them in reverse order; the two shorter letters will give an insight into the sort of situation that prompted the fuller teaching of the first epistle.

These notes, which will take us through the coming fortnight, are intended to be used with any modern edition of the Bible.

7–13 DECEMBER 3 & 2 JOHN; 1 JOHN 1:1—2:27

1 Tension and mission *Read 3 John*

From the very start this short letter draws us into a world of strong Christian friendships—and sharp disagreements. We meet four rather different personalities.

- '**The Elder**' (v. 1) writes this letter; his name is also on the second epistle. Is this the same 'Elder John' who was remembered in the second century as one of the fathers of Christianity in the Ephesus region? Is he also the apostle John, who followed Jesus? We can guess, but we cannot be sure. I shall call him John, although the three Epistles themselves do not mention his name. Evidently he has influence and authority in Christian circles, extending well beyond his own immediate locality.
- **Gaius** (v. 1) is a common name; four Christians in the New Testament have it. John looks on Gaius both as a 'child' (v. 4), a spiritual dependant, and as an ally in a difficult situation. He asks him to give hospitality to a group of travelling Christian workers, and to send them on their way 'in a manner worthy of God' (vv. 5–8).
- **Diotrephes** (v. 9) appears to be a church leader in the area where Gaius lives. He has flouted John's authority, and has stopped the local Christians from giving hospitality to itinerant preachers whom John sends out. John is no longer willing to tolerate this conduct, and means to challenge Diotrephes—when he can get there to do so (v. 10). In the meantime he wants to make other provision for the missionaries; if some in the local church are blocking their coming, because of the headstrong and contentious leadership of Diotrephes, then John must find another way of advancing the gospel.
- **Demetrius** (v. 12) may very well be one of the group John is sending to Gaius. Perhaps he is the person who carries the letter. Obviously he is someone whom John can trust.

So behind the personalities are serious issues. Mission is one: the spread of the faith depends on the support of Christians; if we cannot be in the frontline of evangelism ourselves, we can probably do something to help those who are. Disagreement is another: ours is not the first generation to argue about Christianity, but when leaders cannot contain their disputes, these will tend to weaken the church and impede its work. The tension between local congregation and wider church is a hardy perennial: we always depend heavily on local initiative, but the spirit of Diotrephes 'who likes to be prominent' (v. 9) will eventually cause deeper problems than any it solves.

Behind all of this is what John calls 'the truth' (vv. 3, 4, 8): Christianity is not ours to order as we will, either in New Testament times or now. A faith and a way of life have been given to us from Jesus Christ. The health of our church, our mission and our own lives depends on keeping to the pattern given. That is what John means when he writes to Gaius, 'it is well with your soul' (v. 2). His loves to hear of younger Christians who 'walk in the truth' (v. 4), and that is also the great burden of the other two letters—to which we shall turn next.

2 Truth at stake *Read 2 John*

The 'elect lady and her children' (v. 1) are probably a local Christian congregation and its members, so that the 'elect sister' at the end of the letter (v. 13) will be the church from which John writes. This letter, like the third epistle, has to tackle a difficult situation—but we only discover that about halfway through.

First John turns to the basics of the Christian life. Christian truth, the 'truth' on which he laid so much emphasis in the third epistle, both unites and endures. It binds Christians in love (v. 1) and it lasts for ever (v. 2). So Christians who are joined by the truth should follow the command of Christ, and commit themselves to loving one another (vv. 5–6). John is appealing to the bonds of Christian belief and practical care that he shares with his readers; they will need to be clear in their Christian commitments if they are to cope wisely with new pressures that have arisen.

There has been a challenge to 'the truth'. Some members of the churches have 'gone out' (v. 7): certainly they have left the fellowship, and perhaps they have also 'gone out' as missionaries, to spread their beliefs. They may want support from the churches, but their teaching has become such a distortion of Christianity that John resists their claim. Here, he says, is the sort of arch-deceit that deserves the title Antichrist; 'anti' is Greek for 'instead of', so John thinks that this teaching actually tends to supplant the message of Jesus Christ. To help such work, even in a casual and occasional way, might undo the results of a good deal of careful labour (vv. 8, 10, 11).

The opponents' ideas probably seemed 'advanced' (v. 9) to some people, but John reckons them a harmful influence. He is keen to keep them well away from his own flock. So this letter inverts the perspective of the third epistle. There are travellers around, but this time they are not to be welcomed—which is what Diotrephes had said about John's men. We are looking at a mirror image of the other letter.

What is fresh in this epistle is that John gives a brief doctrinal explanation: the people he opposes 'deny Jesus as Christ come in the flesh'. The reasons for the sharp warnings of this short letter will become clearer as we read the detail of 1 John. Yet 2 John plainly says that shared belief in Jesus Christ and practical Christian love create strong bonds of unity, and that there is no very real spiritual fellowship without these. Perhaps that has been your experience too.

3 A touching place *Read 1 John 1:1–4*

If you could take one Christian doctrine to a desert island…? It's a foolish question, because our faith hangs together as an integrated whole, and we cannot separate one part from the others. Yet sometimes we do need to recall one particular piece of Christian truth, in order to hold our balance through a disturbing period of life.

John stresses the incarnation, the en-flesh-ment of the very life of God, as the message of the moment for his own readers. He says 'we': 'we heard, we saw, we looked on, we touched with our hands'. This is language of personal encounter, the church's recollection of Jesus Christ, living as one of us, yet bearing in himself the very life of God.

I reckon this must be John's own memory, and possibly that of others in his fellowship. At the very least it is the shared memory of his church, their family heritage as a Christian company, that they find their life in the name of Jesus, who was both eternal Son of God and human flesh. They look back to his time on earth, not as to a distant world, but to a person whom men and women had seen and touched. They know that the personal links between that life and their own are close enough to say 'we'. The Christian message is already 'old' (see 2:7); there is a firm and clear tradition. Yet the roots of the message are not lost beyond the horizon of personal connection.

This opening to the epistle is so very like the beginning of John's Gospel that many people find a strong connection between the two. Indeed this is only one of many echoes and similarities between gospel and epistle. The coming of God's own presence, the sharing of God's own life in human flesh, will be a repeated emphasis in the epistle, as it is a cardinal idea in the gospel.

John grounds his message in the incarnation. That is his primary emphasis, that the Son of God shared our humanity. This might also be your doctrine for a desert island; but it is not an insular message, for it connects our lives with countless other Christians, in fellowship with the Father, and with his Son Jesus Christ.

4 Not perfect, just pardoned *Read 1 John 1:5—2:6*

Light and darkness provide a further echo of the prologue to John's Gospel (compare John 1:4, 5, 9). To 'walk in the light' (v. 7) means a serious endeavour to follow and copy God's own light, the life of Jesus. It also means an honesty about ourselves: in God's light we shall be able to recognize and confess our failures. So John's repeated 'if we say' (1:6, 8, 10) and 'anyone who says' (2:4, 6) strike two different emphases.

Firstly, Christian life should be marked by meaningful obedience to the commands of Christ; that is a sign of its reality (2:3). The person who claims to know Jesus Christ, but whose living does not show this relationship, cannot be taken seriously (2:4). John never spells out the commands of Christ in detail, but he summarizes them in two ways: imitation, to 'walk as Christ walked' (2:6); and love, which will be the main theme of 2:7–11.

The second emphasis comes in the final verses of chapter 1. The Christian who claims to be perfect should not be taken seriously either. Sin remains a problem for Christians, as our record and the inner recesses of our character can bear witness. To overlook our sin is to play false with ourselves and with the grace of God (1:8, 10); when we confess it, we discover the forgiveness and inner renewal for which Christ died.

What was the problem in John's church—with its 'advanced' Christians (2 John 9) who had left and who may have attracted others? Were there some who thought themselves perfect, needing no forgiveness? Had they overlooked the basics of Christian obedience and love?

Whatever the circumstances that prompted John's message, this double emphasis points to the pendulum of a healthy Christian life. When we know God's gracious forgiveness, that is a powerful stimulus towards godly living; and if we aim steadily for a godly way of life, we shall often discover that we still need to be forgiven.

5 Morning has broken *Read 1 John 2:7–17*

The theme of light continues. For John the light of God is a light of hope, a bright promise to overcome the dark values which shape so much of the world's living. This darkness 'is passing away' (v. 8). Its grip is weakening. Christians are to live by the new way that Jesus Christ has brought into the world. The love command is old, and new (vv. 7–8). It is as old as the Old Testament (Leviticus 19:18), yet is given a new vitality by Jesus (John 13:34). For the readers too, this command has the familiarity of time, yet is always to be lived afresh in the encounters of each day.

Love is the key. In a splintering and separating church, John stresses this cohesive Christian virtue, as a hallmark of true Christianity, a sign that Christ's light is among them (vv. 9–11). He contrasts it with 'love for the world', our human desire for pleasure, property and prominence. These are passing and shallow treasures, of temporary value only (v. 16). A text like this invites us to consider what we really love: possessions, position—or people?

The middle section of our passage (vv. 12–14) is rather cryptic: what does it mean, and how does it connect with the verses around? Probably these verses outline the marks of a sound

Christian life, the spiritual basis on which John wants his readers to resist the pull of the world. Knowledge of our forgiveness; strength to resist evil; deep acquaintance with God: these are qualities to give resolve to the Christian. John may be thinking of different stages in our life, when he writes to 'little children, fathers and young men'; but he may also mean that 'all Christians are (by grace, not nature) children in innocence … young men in strength, and fathers in experience' (C.H. Dodd).

6 Urgent times *Read 1 John 2:18–27*

John is speaking now of the people who left his church, those of whom we heard in the second epistle. He doubts whether they are genuine Christians; their leaving is a sign of dubious commitment (v. 19). Indeed, if they deny that Jesus is God's Christ, then their version of religion is actually anti-Christian, for it obstructs and obscures the gospel proper (v. 22).

These people may be drifting away from Christianity towards Judaism, believing that Jesus was not really God's messiah at all. Or (a more favoured explanation) they may be distorting Christianity, by taking such an exalted view of God's Christ as to think that he could not truly become human; he might just have alighted upon the man Jesus for a while. Either way they did not recognize Jesus as God incarnate on earth; they would not have agreed that 'the word became flesh' (John 1:14).

John feels that this sort of challenge to the faith brings conflict and urgency with it. It injects tension and momentum into our view of history. It is an advance sign of the final consummation of all things (v. 18).

Yet John writes confidently to his 'little children'. They have God's anointing (vv. 20, 27), a touch of the Holy Spirit, sealing and securing the message of the gospel in their lives. There is probably a deliberate play on words: the word 'Christ' means 'anointed', so the anointing that Christians receive from God brings them into the company of Jesus Christ. Their faith in him creates fellowship with God (v. 23), and this stretches forward into eternal life (vv. 24–25). They need not be led on to further and deeper beliefs, they need only keep steady in the truth they already have. What they have held 'from the beginning' of their Christian lives (v. 24) will hold them in fellowship with God, who is absolutely 'from the beginning' (1:1).

GUIDELINES

The first letter of John is difficult territory to map. The argument spirals, often returning to themes previously touched. Much that we have read this week we shall meet again. Yet two themes come especially in this week's portion, both from chapter 1.

- ***Fellowship:*** *We have fellowship with God, with Jesus, and with the whole Christian Church, because God shared fellowship with us, in the life of Jesus (1:3).*
- ***Forgiveness:*** *Christians need it too. Sin always divides. Pardon unites us, with the whole Church, in the light of God, through the death of Jesus (1:7).*

Lord Jesus Christ,
in the flesh of your human life you shared fellowship with us;
by the blood of your holy death we find forgiveness in you,
that your Spirit may abide in us and we in you. Amen.

14–20 DECEMBER — 1 JOHN 2:28—5:21

The epistles of John have taken us into a scattered group of fairly new churches. There has been a split, and new leadership has broken away. From one point of view the letters simply portray a quarrel between an elderly leader and some younger Christians with new ideas. Some modern readers of the letters are sceptical: why should we take one side, rather than the other? Why sympathize with the writer, and not with his opponents?

My answer to that is twofold. First, John wants to keep the churches in touch with the roots and basis of their faith. He nails his colours to the mast of the incarnation. The life of God took human nature, in the man Jesus. Jesus was truly flesh, yet in an ordinary and accessible human life he revealed 'that which was from the beginning'. This is both a means of contact, of 'fellowship' between people and God, and also a stimulus to a loving and godly way of life. If God so lived, if God so loved, so ought we.

So John's strategy is 'apostolic': he wants to ground the church in the doctrine of its founding generation. This is how we have known Jesus, he argues. The faith is not ours to change, and if we do change it, we shall find that it loses its power to stir and shape our living.

My second reason for supporting John is his emphasis on love. True, he is contending for his beliefs, and has used some harsh words. Yet the love on which he places so much stress is a uniting force. The drive and novelty of his opponents' ideas may have attracted attention, but no church will flourish for long on ideas alone. John values Christian relationships and the love which holds them together.

So we may rightly listen to John. He was a leader in touch with the past, genuinely concerned for a faith that would reflect what God had done in Jesus. He was also concerned for the future, keen that his 'children' sustain their fellowship, in the love that Jesus had given to them.

1 Family likeness *Read 1 John 2:28—3:10*

In the opening verses of today's portion, John looks forward to the 'appearing' of Jesus Christ (2:28), what Christians have sometimes called the second coming. He does not portray it as a great drama, but as a family reunion.

For Christians are God's children, but that is a secret identity for the moment. In the everyday life of the world there is no obvious outer sign to mark this inner reality. Christianity is often an anonymous faith, for we live by the name of Jesus but are not recognized by that name. John expects that, for the world did not acknowledge Jesus either (3:1).

Yet John writes of a bright hope, that the Church will one day see Jesus. There will be a coming together of the Lord and his followers. All weariness and darkness will recede into the background, 'for we shall see him as he is' (v. 2).

John expects that message to encourage the church in faithful living. This hope of family reunion ought to strengthen them, so that they live more truly by their Christian identity. They are 'born of God' (v. 9), and God's own life is in them; that life must come out, in pure and righteous conduct (vv. 3, 7). Again John does not list the fine detail of Christian behaviour. He is not aiming to teach new duties; he wants to hold his people to their existing commitment. All the detail he needs to give is summed up in the love command—which will be the theme of tomorrow's portion.

John's strong language about sin and righteousness has disturbed some readers, for example, verse 6. We recall what John wrote in 1:8–9; we know that we are not fully and finally clear of sin. So what is he saying in 3:6, and where does that leave us?

The best explanation is that we 'cannot avoid the fact of sin, but we can avoid its practice' (S. Smalley). We are indeed tripped up at times by weakness and temptation. That is shameful, but inevitable, and we must seek God's forgiveness—as 1:8–9 explains. However, when we shape our habits, plan our days and determine our commitments, we are called to follow the new identity that is ours in Christ. Sin may impose its company upon us, but it has no claim on our hospitality. That is the message of 3:6.

So let us pause to reflect on John's hope—not a hope to make us casual or complacent, nor a hope to prompt endless speculation about dates and schemes, but a hope to animate us, to help us confirm in practical ways our new identity in Christ. The promise that we shall see Jesus as he is, and shall then be most truly and fully ourselves, is still part of the faith, and is still an incentive in the Christian life.

2 The love affair *Read 1 John 3:11–18*

Biologists talk about 'characteristics of life': movement, growth, respiration and so on, the features that distinguish living creatures from inanimate objects. If you asked John about the characteristics of Christian life, he would put love high on the list. 'We know we have crossed from death into life, because we love our brothers and sisters' (v. 14).

John sees a deep spiritual division in the world, between God's children and the people whose lives are governed by evil (v. 10). He uses the ancient story of Cain and Abel (v. 12; from Genesis 4), to illustrate how very bitter the quarrels in the world can be. Hatred, says John, is a murderous and sterile thing (v. 15; compare Jesus, in Matthew 5:21–22). The Christian family is called to something very different, to a practical, observant, and sacrificial love, a fellowship of open eyes, open hearts and open hands (vv. 16–18).

By way of aside at this point, notice how many turns of phrase in this epistle echo passages from John's Gospel. For example, in just a few verses of Chapter 3:

- *'Born of God' (v. 10) contrasts 'children of the devil'; as in John 3:3 and 8:44.*
- *The love command (v. 11) echoes John 13:34.*
- *'The world hates you' (v. 13) is what Jesus told his disciples (John 15.18).*
- *'Lay down your lives' (v. 16) is what Jesus did for his friends (John 15:13).*

There are other matching expressions throughout the epistle, enough to indicate a strong connection with the gospel. We may well be dealing with the same author, although some scholars prefer to think of two different authors, from a single Christian community. Admittedly, the ideas in John and 1 John are not identical: for example the significant term 'seed' (v. 9) does not appear in the gospel, and the word 'glory', which is quite important in the gospel, is missing from the epistle.

But there are links of some kind. Which of the two was written first? No one knows. If the gospel came first, then the epistle probably deliberately echoes material from it. If the epistle was first, it may well be using Christian teaching which the churches knew, teaching which was written down later as part of the gospel.

So there are tantalizing mysteries around this letter: it seems to claim personal memories of Jesus; it exudes an aura of seniority and authority in matters of faith. If the epistle is not by John the apostle (and possibly it is not), then no one knows for sure who wrote it. And if the gospel is not by the author of the epistle, it probably uses a lot of that author's material; it may have been written out in final form after his death (as John 21:23–24 might suggest).

3 The heart of the matter *Read 1 John 3:19—4:6*

Many people find trouble with the question of assurance. How can I know that I am a Christian? How can I be sure that the life of Jesus Christ is in me? Once we start that train of thought, feelings can be an unreliable barometer, and we may find that 'our heart condemns us' (v. 20); we do not feel truly and properly new.

John tackles the same issue. There has been a split in the church, and varying opinions are around. He wants his friends to recognize true Christianity in their own lives. If the signs are present, then they need not worry or be drawn away. An uneasy heart is not the best indicator for sorting this question out, but 'God is greater than our heart, and knows everything' (v. 20). A right perspective in this matter has two focal points: belief in Jesus, and love (v. 23). These are the two basic tests.

So the first mark of Christian life is belief in 'Jesus, as Christ come in the flesh' (4:2). He was not merely human, but he was truly human. He was not God distant from earth, but God present on earth. He was heaven's communication with earth, and our human contact with the life of God. Christians who believe that need not modify their faith in search of something fuller or more spiritual. All we need to know about God comes out of that doctrine; everything else that is important connects with it.

This brings us to the Holy Spirit, the inner presence of God in the life of the believer. 'We know God's abiding in us,' says John, 'by the Spirit he has given us' (3:24). This is roughly what Paul says: 'The Spirit witnesses with our spirit that we are children of God' (Romans 8:16). The Spirit is an inner assurance for the Christian.

Yet because different groups are claiming to represent the true spirit of Christianity, John also writes, 'Test the spirits' (4:1). One prime test is that the Holy Spirit of God will always promote belief in Jesus. A Christian who has that faith need not doubt where it comes from.

4 Love that flows, love that shows *Read 1 John 4:7–21*

Two cardinal signs of Christian life were mentioned in 3:23—belief, and love. In these coming verses John writes about love, and links it tightly to what he has just said about faith. Love does not start with us. It comes to us, from outside ourselves: 'God sent his Son, that we might live' (v. 9). Love comes from the incarnation, from the coming of Jesus into the world.

The coming led to the cross, where Jesus took the guilt of human wrongdoing on himself, 'a sacrifice for our sins' (v. 10). That too was a work of love, not a narrow exchange, a calculation of guilt and debt alone, but a love-gift from God to a wayward and needy world. So a Christian life, nourished by faith in Jesus, is richly supplied with love. We are now to give that love out, as a daily reflection of the love of the Lord, whose own life dwells in us (v. 11).

In many a town centre or public park there is a fountain, which overflows constantly with sparkling cool water—as surely as the overflow of love in a generous Christian life. But a fountain works from an external water supply, which must be sufficient to power it, and must never dry up—as we depend on the love of God, which comes to us through the death of Christ.

If we know and show his love, we shall not be afraid of God (v. 18), nor of the future (v. 17). Our brothers and sisters in Christ will gain strength from us. For love is a visual aid; it displays God's presence (v. 12).

5 Calm on the battle *Read 1 John 5:1–5*

John writes a lot about love for 'brothers', for other Christians. His first concern is to steady the Christian ship, after internal disturbance; he talks about relationships within the church, because these are under stress. The love he commends will need to overcome envy, to repair tensions, and mend fences within the fellowship—for every sharp difference and division leaves rough edges behind.

What then about love for people outside the Christian fold? John's Gospel certainly tells of love for the unlovely. God loved the world, and Jesus Christ came to express that love (John 3:16). The same worldwide perspective shows in this epistle, at 1 John 2:2. God's love can both heal the damage in the church, and also shape the sort of approachable and caring Christian character which will commend Christ to people outside.

However, there are tense relations with outsiders. 'The world hates you,' says John (1 John 3:13). Possibly these Christians had been cold-shouldered by family and former friends, so that they had come to depend heavily on each other in times of material need. Practical love within the Christian company has become a pressing and urgent matter.

So John writes of 'overcoming the world' (vv. 4–5). His friends may have been under severe pressure. They were pulled too by the world's values and way of life (recall 2:15–17), all the more tempting when the Christian way was difficult and the church divided. They must have felt a sense of conflict, almost as if they were living on a battlefield.

In our own time, the attitudes other people adopt do not always allow the church to meet them with active love. Some Christians nowadays face severe opposition for their faith. Yet Christians may respond to hostility with gentleness, persistent faith, and mutual care. That is a victory to which the people of Jesus are always called, even when the world misunderstands and dislikes the Christian way.

6 Life assurance *Read 1 John 5:6–21*

Perhaps your Bible has a footnote at verse 7. The mention of 'the Father, the Word and the Holy Ghost' is nicely theological and gives a parallel to the 'three witnesses' in verse 8, but it is not in the earliest manuscripts of the epistle and is surely not from John's hand. We think it was slipped in about AD300, possibly in Spain. The actual text of the New Testament was usually quite carefully copied, and well preserved. There are not many places where such a lengthy (and doubtless well-meant) insertion has persisted to appear in the text of printed Bibles. Now that its dubious origin is known, many twentieth-century Bibles leave it out.

So the cryptic wording of verse 8 must go with verse 6. Jesus came by the poured water of his baptism, and the shed blood of his cross. At baptism he came to Israel, and in his coming he received the Spirit (John 1:31–34). On the cross he left his friends, and in his going he gave the Spirit (John 16:7). Water and blood are remembered in the Christian sacraments of baptism and communion, and in both of these sacraments the church still seeks the Spirit's presence. For the Holy Spirit is a double witness, to the life that Jesus lived as God's anointed servant, and to the death that he died in fulfilling that service. In both these moments, in his action and in his passion, he was God's Son. The cross, painful, miserable, humiliating, and shameful as it was, is part of God's witness to his Son (v. 9). The God we serve is a humble God, of sacrificial and outgoing love.

So the church may be confident in the love of God. That love has given us eternal life, in Jesus Christ (v. 11). The message of the letter is summed up in verse 13—just as John 20:31 sums up the purpose of the gospel. John Stott comments on those two key verses: 'Putting together the purposes of Gospel and Epistle, John's purpose is in four stages, that his readers should hear, hearing should believe, believing should live, and living should know.' The epistle concentrates on the last of those four aims. Amid confusing and disturbing pressures, Christians are to 'know that you have eternal life' (v. 13).

The epistle ends by encouraging the church to pray (vv. 14–15), and to keep a loving watch over one another (v. 16). John reminds his friends of the spiritual security they have through what God has done for them in Jesus (vv. 18–20). Remain in that truth, is his message. Avoid the enticements of other beliefs and teachings (v. 21).

GUIDELINES

For those who like a mystery, the epistles of John are full of riddles. Who wrote them, when, and where? How do gospel and epistles belong together? There is much of which we cannot be sure. Yet John's own message is one of firm spiritual assurance. He delights to tell his friends about the lasting gift of God's love, in the life and death of Jesus.

He repeats his main command over and again, coming to the same point from different angles and in different ways, writing with the conviction of experience, in the patient wisdom of a pastor. Love one another. Faith will be steady, faith will be sustained, faith will be shown, if Christians will live in love, love which they have received through the coming and the cross of Jesus Christ.

Thanks be to thee, my Lord Jesus Christ,
for all the benefits thou hast given to me,
for all the pains and insults which thou hast borne for me.
O most merciful redeemer, friend and brother,
may I know thee more clearly,
love thee more dearly,
and follow thee more nearly,
day by day. Amen.

Richard of Chichester's Prayer

Further reading

John's epistles are very well supplied with commentaries. Some of these are very detailed indeed. Four recent authors offer compact treatments, which still deal with this short text in a clear and helpful way. The fifth title, by Judith Lieu, discusses the letters theme by theme, rather than chapter by chapter. Smalley's excellent commentary is for those who want something bigger.

Thomas F. Johnson, *1, 2 and 3 John*, New International Biblical Commentary, Hendrickson 1993.

William Loader, *The Johannine Epistles*, Epworth Preachers' Commentary, 1992.

John R.W. Stott, *The Epistles of John*, Tyndale Commentary, IVP, revised edition 1988.

Marion Meye Thompson, *1–3 John*, New Testament Commentary, IVP 1992.

Judith Lieu, *The Theology of the Johannine Epistles*, CUP 1991.

Stephen S. Smalley, *1, 2, 3 John*, Word Biblical Commentary 1984.

Christmas Readings

The readings for the next eleven days cover familiar ground, but at the same time expose some features of the landscape that are easily missed. The Christmas story is full of reassurance and hope in its celebration of the coming of Immanuel, 'God with us'. But there is a disturbing side to all this. Jesus is born among the world's lowly people. His birth is greeted with suspicion, dismay, brutality. And the story that puts the child at the centre issues a call to a discipleship which is prepared to rearrange received wisdom.

The readings can be used with any version of the Bible.

21–27 DECEMBER

1 The Jubilee *Read Isaiah 61*

Like Advent, the Jewish New Year, Rosh ha-Shanah, which is celebrated in the autumn, is marked by the theme of judgment. Today's reading picks up that theme, appropriate for the approaching end of the year and our contemplation of the millennium. Our reading is one that proclaims the hope of Jubilee and at the same time 'the day of vengeance of our God', and forms the context of the start of Jesus' public ministry according to Luke 4:18ff. It contains a theme which has formed an important part of the churches' preparation for the year 2000. In the campaign Jubilee 2000 many Christians are seeking the remission of Third World debt.

The prophet comes to a situation of mourning and ruins (vv. 3 and 4) and offers hope. There is also a role hitherto reserved for a priestly élite to a downtrodden people ('you shall be called priests of the Lord', v. 6). This hope is based on a God who loves justice and will cause righteousness and praise to spring up before all nations (vv. 8 and 11). The confident tone of these beautiful words strikes a dissonant chord as we shrink from such defiant and hopeful proclamation in a society which cares little for God's justice. We imagine that it must have been so different then. In some ways it was, but in respect of the despair and the lack of evidence of the signs and practice of the divine justice, the situation of the unknown prophet of the exile who uttered these words is little changed. It demands of those who follow to repeat that message of hope and the practice which can make it a reality.

2 The unconventional genealogy of Jesus *Read Matthew 1:1–17*

When we begin the Christmas story in Matthew's Gospel we usually start with 1:16. Perhaps we should, for a change, start at the very beginning. There we shall find that Matthew's is not described as a gospel but as a *book* of the genesis of Jesus Christ. The genealogy stresses that Jesus is the true child of Abraham and David, themes which are to appear again later in 3:9 and 22:41ff. The most telling feature of this list of names, so easily missed, is the inclusion of reference to four women (vv. 3, 5, 6), plus Mary in verse 18, an interesting feature compared with Luke 3:23ff, which includes only men. Then all of the women who appear in the list are hardly conventional figures either untouched by scandal or the paragons of what passes in society for virtue. There is Tamar in verse 3, abused by her father-in-law (Genesis 38); Ruth the Moabitess who was ancestor of David; Rahab the prostitute; Bathsheba, not named in verse 6, whose husband Uriah's death had been brutally arranged by David. Then, finally, there is Mary, unmarried and pregnant, and yet whose child is of the Holy Spirit. The neat assumptions about what counts as legitimacy before God and our expectations of how God might choose to act, or where God's presence might be found, are disturbed by this genealogy, just as the story of Jesus in the pages of Matthew's book which follow will disturb the neat conventions and patterns of life.

The themes of Matthew's first two chapters, the surprising character of Jesus' birth in obscurity and his persecution by the powerful, are continued as the gospel begins its account of Jesus' mission, which starts with the message of an eccentric prophet in the desert. It is not in Jerusalem that Jesus settles but the margins of Israel's life (4:16, cf. Isaiah 9:1). It is here that the proclamation of the imminence of God's reign begins with the healing of every kind of disease (4:23f). At its opening Matthew presents a story of God's messiah who is greeted with suspicion and dismay, and is persecuted by those in power. Born in an apparently insignificant place, identifying with those regarded as sinners, taking children as examples of the attitude of humility appropriate for the kingdom, Jesus' unconventional message echoes his unconventional genealogy, and is exemplified in the character of those who are blessed at the beginning of the Sermon on the Mount.

From the beginning, the story of Jesus is one in which the reversal of values and priorities and the undermining of conventional hierarchy are central. It is the rulers who misunderstand and mislead the crowd; the demon-possessed and outsiders rather than the 'normal' who glimpse Jesus' true character. 'The last will be first, and the first will be last' (Matthew 20:16).

3 Immanuel *Read Matthew 1:18–25*

Jesus' genesis in verse 18 needs to be explained. Matthew, like Luke, needs to put the record straight (cf. Luke 1:4). Joseph is the focus of attention in his infancy story, whereas in Luke 1:26ff the attention is on Mary. Joseph shows himself to be a true son of David (v. 20), a righteous man. He stands in stark contrast with Herod who was the king in Jerusalem but who, as we read in yesterday's passage, forms no part of the genealogy of the messiah. Joseph could have rid himself of Mary (cf. Deuteronomy 22:20), but was responsive to the angelic vision and set aside his initial decision to divorce Mary quietly. We find throughout this gospel that the way of God may be discerned through dreams (1:20; 2:13; 2:19; 27:19), a reminder of their importance for understanding individual and social life for many people, modern as well as ancient (we are reminded of this in the book of Daniel, e.g. Daniel 2).

Immanuel, God with us, appears in unusual circumstances. The hidden appearance of the divine emerges later in the gospel, where two or three are gathered together in the name of Jesus (18:20), in the persons of the hungry, the thirsty, the stranger, the naked, the ill and the imprisoned (25:35ff). There the heavenly Son of Man meets us. Christ, God with us, comes in the least expected persons and places.

4 Meditation and crisis *Read John 1:1–18*

These sonorous words, which have become such an important part of the Christmas season, contain some of the most profound and complex theology in the New Testament. Here we find within, at most, a couple of generations of Jesus' life, a writer indicating the oneness of the Word with God. That divine Word became flesh in the person of Jesus of Nazareth.

The opening verses of John's Gospel are a mixture of sublime metaphysics and down-to-earth history. The person of John the Baptist, so important as a solitary witness to Jesus on the margins of a nation's life, interrupts this meditation on God's eternal purposes. John's is a voice which needs to be heeded, because this eccentric prophet perceived the presence of the Word become flesh (1:29). The note of judgment which is at the centre of John's message in the synoptic gospels (e.g. Matthew 3:7ff) recurs in these well-known verses too. The light is not welcomed. The coming one knocks, but the door is not opened (cf. Revelation 3:20). Rather he comes to his own (and still does), and his own did not receive him. The gaudy sentimentalities of Christmas glitter are shot through with the spectre of judgment and rejection. The gospel of the righteousness of God provokes not sweetness and light but a crisis for the individual and the world.

5 The birth of Jesus *Read Luke 2:1–20*

This beautiful passage, which speaks of the extraordinary manifestation of the angelic world at the time of the birth of Jesus, is quite remarkable within the gospels. As in Matthew, the peculiar circumstances of Jesus' birth need to be explained by divine revelation (Luke 1:26, cf. Matthew 1:20). Who might have expected the messiah to appear in such humble surroundings?

The attendance of the heavenly host in the ordinary circumstances of a human birth set this humble woman and her child apart. Just as in Isaiah 6, where the prophet is brought into the glory of the heavenly court with the seraphim lauding God in the temple, and in the vision of John of Patmos in Revelation 4, where the prophet catches a glimpse of the divine throne and the slaughtered Lamb, our Lucan reading portrays the angelic host singing the praises of God. But they appear neither in temple nor in heaven (v. 13) but with a group of herdsmen at night (v. 8) on a Judean hillside. The mundane circumstances of the demonstration of God's glory are consistent with themes evident throughout the gospels. The divine is located in unexpected places, among the lowly and pre-eminently in the humiliated Son of God: 'Lord, when was it that we saw you hungry and fed you, thirsty and gave you drink, stranger and took you home, or naked and clothed you? … Inasmuch as you have done it for the least of these you have done it for me' (Matthew 25:37, 40).

6 The story of Stephen *Read Acts 6:8—7:1; 7:34–53 (6:8—8:1 if you have time)*

Do *you* celebrate the life and death of St Stephen in the depth of the Christmas season ? His feast day is hidden away on Boxing Day, arguably now the most secular day of the year. As a result the most radical voice in the New Testament is hardly ever heard.

According to Acts, the first Christians continued to worship in the temple but, as the years went on, the temple became a metaphor for the holiness and sense of divine presence in the world in the lives of men, women and children. They became disengaged from the bricks and trappings of a finely decorated building. The importance of the physical temple diminished, particularly in those texts which now form the canon of our New Testament. Recall the Johannine Jesus' words: 'The hour is coming when you will worship the Father neither on this mountain nor in Jerusalem … the true worshippers will worship the Father in spirit and truth, for the Father seeks such as these to worship him' (John 4:21, 23).

Among the earliest voices raised about the need for this change of understanding is that of Stephen. He was thought to have said harsh words against the temple (Acts 6:13f), and his implicit criticism of the temple, which comes at the climax of the long speech at his trial, led to his death (7:54ff). In the speech attributed to him in Acts 7 he dwells on the rebelliousness of the majority of his ancestors. Note the way, in verses 42 and 46, the period in the wilderness is seen as an abandonment of God's way, sentiments reminiscent of Ezekiel's telling of the story of the people of God in Ezekiel 20:35. In his review of Israel's history he points to Solomon's act in building the temple as a departure from the divine intention. He built a house for God, which, if the quotation from Isaiah 66:1 in Acts 8:49–50 is anything to go by, suggests that such an enterprise completely missed the point of worship of almighty God: 'Yet the Most High does not dwell in houses made with human hands; as the prophet says, "Heaven is my throne, and the earth is my footstool. What kind of house will you build for me, says the Lord, or what is the place of my rest? Did not my hand make all these things?"' What God intended was a dwelling place for the 'house of Jacob' (v. 46—note how some manuscripts followed by the Revised English Bible prefer 'God of Jacob', which suggests that God *did* approve of the building of the temple). Yet Solomon built a house for God, not a dwelling place for Jacob/Israel.

That encapsulation of the service of almighty God in the permanent building rather than the portable tabernacle is rejected by Stephen, the spiritual radical, who explains to his hearers that the Lord does not place a high value on stones and buildings. It is good to be reminded of that in the middle of the Christmas season when sentiment runs riot and Christianity is equated with decorated churches, carols, and a heady mix of nostalgia. True religion means 'to do justice, to love kindness and to walk humbly with your God' (Micah 6:8).

GUIDELINES

The story of Jesus demands of us a rearrangement of received wisdom according to different principles and concerns. It reflects the unexpectedness of God's acts, the way they challenge conventional assumptions about social status. The negative reaction of the politically powerful to Jesus comes as no surprise, therefore. Jesus offers a vision of divine kingship in his activity, in the way he ministered to persons of little account in the society of his day. This kingship does not involve force for arms (Matthew 26:52f, cf. John 18:36), but humility and compassion.

To be a disciple means identifying with the child (Matthew 18:2). In Matthew 18 the disciples ask Jesus who is the greatest in the kingdom of heaven. He answers by taking a child and instructing the disciples to become like that child. Response to the child or the little one is the same as response to Jesus. Just as fulfilling the needs of the hungry and the thirsty means doing it to the heavenly Son of Man, so receiving a child means receiving Jesus, the Son of Man (18:5, cf. 25:31ff). The position of children in the ancient world was very different from the (apparently) more child-centred world of today. Children were often treated, by our standards, brutally and callously. In Matthew's Gospel, the child moves to centre stage. It is the birth of a child to humble parents that causes consternation in Jerusalem. Children greet the meek and lowly king as he enters Jerusalem, while the hierarchy look on disdainfully (Matthew 21:15). To place a child in the midst of the disciples is to challenge the assumption that the child has nothing of worth and should only be heeded when it has received an adult's wisdom.

As late twentieth-century people, a child-centred universe may not strike us as being at all strange. And yet how far have we journeyed in our compassion when stories of child-abuse and even our own painful memories of childhood humiliations remind us that being a child is not always a time of enchantment or delight? Too often it may be a matter of being, at best, 'seen and not heard'. Disciples of Jesus are called to become once more like the children they once were, and, despite being adults, to identify with 'the little ones' (18:5), wherever they are to be found.

28–31 DECEMBER

1 Simeon and Anna *Read Luke 2:25–38*

These two old people join the unlikely group of witnesses to the Lord's messiah. For Simeon there is a moment of spiritual intuition as he recognizes the one among so many brought to the temple. One can only wonder what marked this child out. After all, his parents were not obvious candidates for the anointed one, offering only the humblest gifts (v. 24, cf. Leviticus 12:8). Nevertheless it is that discernment which comes from the Spirit, whose inspiration permeates the story of Jesus, not least in the opening chapters of Luke's Gospel. It is the Spirit who brings about the birth of the messiah and inspires the ejaculations of praise and confession. It is a moment of inspiration that leads Simeon to bless God and ask for release. The word used here is of the liberation of a slave. Seeing the child marks the moment of Simeon's deliverance from bondage, which affects the old man because it is political and social. Simeon's words anticipate the revelation of the gospel to the nations (v. 32, picking up on Isaiah 40:5, 52:10; cf. Colossians 1:26). How many would ask for that release from life, something to which we cling, particularly on the very brink of deliverance? (In this, Simeon resembles Moses in Deuteronomy 32:50.)

This poignant moment is shot through with ambiguity, for Jesus is described as a sign of contradiction which will not leave many unaffected. Anna anticipates the women at the tomb and the first Christians in her evangelistic zeal. One can imagine the response to such effusive language about the child of a humble country girl in the metropolis. She speaks to all those awaiting the liberation of Israel. We may note the highly charged political term used here in verse 38 and earlier in verse 29: release/redemption. Peter Selby, Bishop of Worcester, has written: 'There is in Simeon's words something more vibrant and demanding … perhaps more political than translations usually bring out. "Now you are releasing your slave, master, according to your word in peace," he says … this indeed might be an announcement of liberation.' As such, it is parallel to the liberation initiated by God's anointed one in Luke 4:16ff.

2 The circumcision of Jesus *Read Luke 2:19–24*

In telling this story Luke appears anxious to stress the obedience of Jesus' parents to ancestral customs. The piety and devotion of the figures in the infancy narratives is everywhere to be seen: Anna, Zechariah and Simeon, as well as Jesus' parents. For Luke it may have been important, in order to stress the continuity of Christianity with Judaism, to show contemporaries that it was no new-fangled cult but a religion having deep roots in one of the Roman world's most venerated religions. But, in addition, it is part of the picture of followers of Christ in the New Testament working within the structures of the day. This does not mean slavish obedience to the powers that be. They may turn the world upside down but this is done by working within the structure of society as it is. Hence Paul instructs Christians at Rome to be subject to the powers that be but not to be obedient to them. That is something altogether different.

Circumcision became an issue which split early Christianity down the middle, much as the issue of homosexual relations threatens to do in the contemporary church. There must have been those who said, 'What was good enough for Jesus is good enough for us too', as they recalled the story of his circumcision. Paul rejected simple acceptance of the Jewish Law for those Gentiles who accepted the salvation about which Simeon prophesied. He saw that the creation of two kinds of Christians, one group circumcised and the other not, when all are one in Christ, would be a denial of the universal salvation which the messiah brought. So obedience to the law was rejected in favour of obedience to the call of Christ. Such a decision was not achieved without a good deal of conflict (reflected in the account of the Jerusalem Council in Acts 15 and the parallel passage in Galatians 2:1–10, where much more raw emotion is in evidence). Sooner or later, people have to learn to live together, even if they engage in terrible hostilities—whether physical or psychological—before realizing it.

3 Epiphany and passion *Read Matthew 2:1–15*

The magi manifest a different kind of wisdom. They are the people who come from the margins to seek for, and worship, a different kind of king (v. 11, cf. 8:2; 15:25; 28:9, 17). They are the ones who come from east and west to sit down with Israel's ancestors in the kingdom (8:11, cf. Daniel 2:27). Meanwhile the ones who should be able to cannot read the signs of the times (16:3, cf. 21:31), and squabble over their meaning.

King Herod forms no part of Jesus' genealogy. So the question arises: who is the true king of the Jews? (v. 2). The answer given in Matthew's Gospel is that it is not the ruthless tyrant who massacres innocents (2:16ff) but the humble king whose attitude to children is very different (18:2; 19:14). The metropolis, Jerusalem, is disturbed by the news of a rival king (v. 3, cf. 21:10), born in the insignificant Bethlehem (v. 5). All this is a sign of things to come later in the gospel, in the passion narrative.

4 Holy innocents *Read Matthew 2:16–18; Exodus 1*

Rachel, the embodiment of suffering, devastated women, weeps for her children (2:18). We can only imagine the horror of those distraught daughters of Rachel as they saw their infants brutally slaughtered, just as their foremothers witnessed male children killed by a tyrant, jealous of his power and paranoid about the threat to his position, described just before the story of Moses' birth, in Exodus 1:22. It is part of the testimony of weak and defenceless people down the ages that they have been confronted with the systematic cruelty which almost defies contemplation and whose explanation (if that is the right word) lies deep within the lust for and maintenance of power.

Here in Matthew's Gospel, it is not that terrible event which dominates the story; it is Jesus' escape as the result of the angelic visitation (2:13). Superficially it seems that the hero escapes, but not to live happily ever after. There will be no escape, finally, for Jesus. According to the Gospel of John, Mary too joins the daughters of Rachel in witnessing the death of her son, brutally executed by the occupying forces, another mother who laments the loss of a child in the face of colonial oppression (John 19:25–27). Jesus becomes one in a long line of prophets killed by those to whom they are sent (Matthew 23:37). The rulers of Jerusalem, like Egypt and Rome, and the rulers of Nazi Germany, Pol Pot's Cambodia, and Stalin, kill not only the prophets sent by God but ordinary, unassuming innocent people, the destruction of whose lives brave prophets have always denounced.

The Bible Reading Fellowship
Peter's Way, Sandy Lane West, Oxford, OX4 5HG
ISBN 1 84101 007 3

Distributed in Australia by:
Hodder Headline Australia, 10–16 South Street,
Rydalmere, (Locked Bag 386), NSW 2116

Distributed in New Zealand by:
Scripture Union Wholesale, PO Box 760, Wellington

Distributed in South Africa by:
Struik Book Distributors, PO Box 193, Maitland 7405

Publications distributed to more than 60 countries

Acknowledgments
The Revised Standard Version of the Bible, copyright © 1946, 1952, 1971 by the Division of Christian Education of the National Council of the Churches of Christ in the USA.

The New Revised Standard Version of the Bible, copyright © 1989 by the Division of Christian Education of the National Council of the Churches of Christ in the USA.

The Holy Bible, New International Version, copyright © 1973, 1978, 1984 by International Bible Society.

New English Bible copyright © 1970 by permission of Oxford and Cambridge University Presses.

Revised English Bible copyright © 1989, by permission of Oxford and Cambridge University Presses.

p.19 Poem reproduced by permission of Morar Lucas.

Cover photograph: Jon Arnold

Printed in Denmark

SUBSCRIPTIONS

❏ I would like to give a gift subscription (please complete both name and address sections below)

❏ I would like to take out a subscription myself (complete name and address details only once)

❏ Please send me details of 3-year subscriptions

This completed coupon should be sent with appropriate payment to BRF. Alternatively, please write to us quoting your name, address, the subscription you would like for either yourself or a friend (with their name and address), the start date and credit card number, expiry date and signature if paying by credit card.

Gift subscription name ______________________________

Gift subscription address ______________________________

____

______________________________ Postcode ______________

Please send to the above, beginning with the Sept 1998/Jan 1999 issue:

(please tick box)	UK	SURFACE	AIR MAIL
LIVEWIRES	❏ £12.00	❏ £13.50	❏ £15.00
GUIDELINES	❏ £9.60	❏ £10.80	❏ £13.20
NEW DAYLIGHT	❏ £9.60	❏ £10.80	❏ £13.20
NEW DAYLIGHT LARGE PRINT	❏ £15.00	❏ £18.60	❏ £21.00

Please complete the payment details below and send your coupon, with appropriate payment to: **The Bible Reading Fellowship, Peter's Way, Sandy Lane West, Oxford OX4 5HG**

Your name ______________________________

Your address ______________________________

____

______________________________ Postcode ______________

Total enclosed £ __________ (cheques should be made payable to 'BRF')

Payment by cheque ❏ postal order ❏ Visa ❏ Mastercard ❏ Switch ❏

Card number: ☐☐☐☐ ☐☐☐☐ ☐☐☐☐ ☐☐☐☐

Expiry date of card: ☐☐☐☐ Issue number (Switch): ☐☐☐☐

Signature (essential if paying by credit/Switch card) ______________

NB: BRF notes are also available from your local Christian bookshop.

GL0398 The Bible Reading Fellowship is a Registered Charity

This page is intentionally left blank

BIBLE READING RESOURCES PACK

A pack of resources and ideas to help to promote Bible reading in your church is available from BRF. The pack which will be of use at any time during the year includes sample editions of the notes, magazine articles, leaflets about BRF Bible reading resources and much more. Unless you specify the month in which you would like the pack sent, we will send it immediately on receipt of your order. We greatly appreciate your donations towards the cost of producing the pack (without them we would not be able to make the pack available) and we welcome your comments about the contents of the pack and your ideas for future ones.

This coupon should be sent to:

The Bible Reading Fellowship
Peter's Way
Sandy Lane West
Oxford OX4 5HG

Name ____

Address ____

____

______________________________ Postcode ________________

Please send me _____ Bible Reading Resources Pack(s)

Please send the pack now/ in____________ (month).

I enclose a donation for £_______ towards the cost of the pack.

GL0398 The Bible Reading Fellowship is a Registered Charity

This page is intentionally left blank

BRF PUBLICATIONS ORDER FORM

Please ensure that you complete and send off both sides of this order form.

Please send me the following book(s):

		Quantity	Price	Total
3502	Day by Day with Shelagh Brown (*S. Brown*)	_____	£6.99	_____
028	People's Bible Commentary: Nahum–Malachi (*G. Emmerson*)	_____	£7.99	_____
3562	Livewires: LIVE (*R. Sharples*)	_____	£8.99	_____
3563	Livewires: Get Into the Bible (*S. Herbert*)	_____	£3.99	_____
3569	Cracking the Church Cocoon (*M. Watsham/N. Matthews*)	_____	£12.99	_____
016	On the Way to Bethlehem (*H. McDowell*)	_____	£5.99	_____

Total cost of books £ ________

Postage and packing (see over) £ ________

TOTAL £ ________

See over for payment details. All prices are correct at time of going to press, are subject to the prevailing rate of VAT and may be subject to change without prior warning.

NB: All BRF titles are also available from your local Christian bookshop.

GL0398

The Bible Reading Fellowship is a Registered Charity

PAYMENT DETAILS

Please complete the payment details below and send with appropriate payment and completed order form to:

**The Bible Reading Fellowship,
Peter's Way,
Sandy Lane West,
Oxford OX4 5HG**

Name ______________________________

Address ______________________________

____

______________________________ Postcode ______________

Total enclosed £ __________ (cheques should be made payable to 'BRF')

Payment by cheque ❑ postal order ❑ Visa ❑ Mastercard ❑ Switch ❑

Card number: ☐☐☐☐ ☐☐☐☐ ☐☐☐☐ ☐☐☐☐

Expiry date of card: ☐☐☐☐ Issue number (Switch): ☐☐☐☐

Signature (essential if paying by credit/Switch card) ______________________________

POSTAGE AND PACKING CHARGES				
order value	UK	Europe	Surface	Air Mail
£7.00 & under	£1.25	£2.25	£2.25	£3.50
£7.01–£14.99	£3.00	£3.50	£4.50	£6.50
£15.00–£29.99	£4.00	£5.50	£7.50	£11.00
£30.00 & over	free	prices on request		

Alternatively you may wish to order books using the BRF telephone order hotline:
01865 748227

The Bible Reading Fellowship is a Registered Charity